PUB WALKS
IN DEVON

Forty Circular Walks

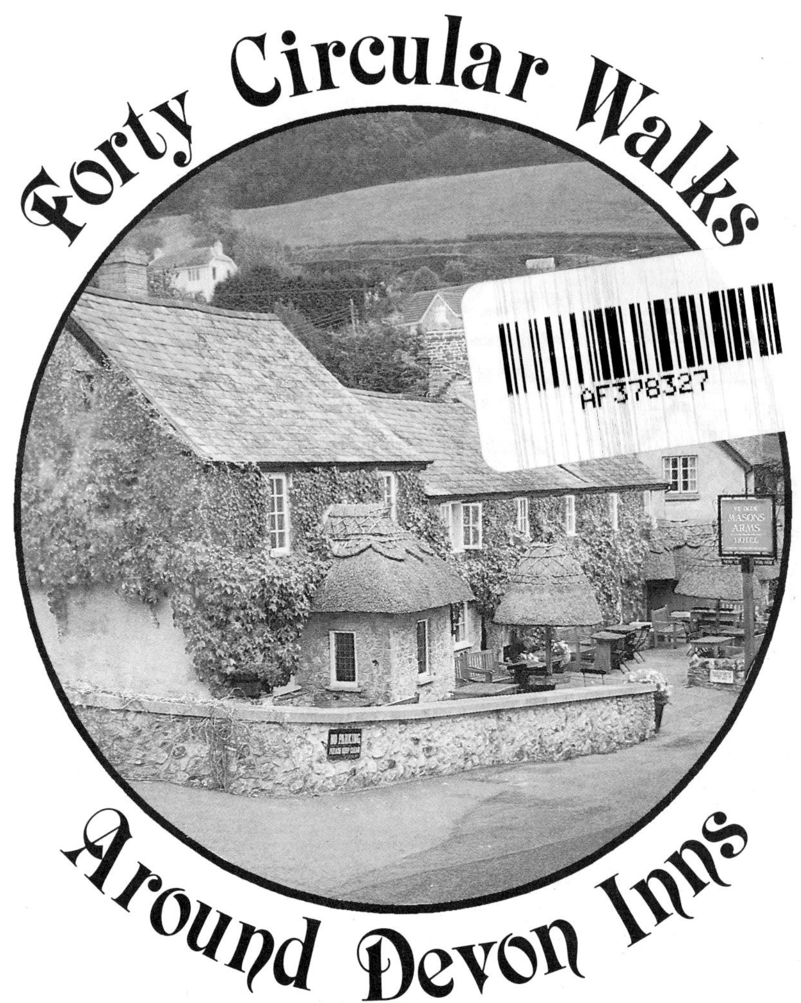

Around Devon Inns

Mike Power

Other Publications in the series.
"Pub Walks in Dorset".
"Forty More Pub Walks in Dorset".
"Pub Walks in Hampshire and the I.O.W."
"Pub Walks in West Sussex".
"Pub Walks in Cornwall".
"The Dorset Coast Path".
"Pub Walks in Kent".
"Pub Walks in East Sussex".

1st edition published January 1993
Reprinted 1995.

Acknowledgements
I would like to thank my wife Cicely for accompanying me on many of my trips into Devon, to the landlord and tenants for their helpful information, to my brother-in-law Ray Vine and Liz Jones who supplied me with two of the photographs.

ISBN 0-9514502-7-1

Publisher's Note
Whilst every care has been taken to ensure the accuracy of all the information given in this book, errors will occur due to many factors. Paths are sometimes re-routed, new stiles and gates are sometimes erected and the pubs frequently change hands. Neither the printer nor the publishers can accept responsibility for any inaccuracies.

Power Publications
1, Clayford Ave, Ferndown
Dorset. BH22 9PQ

Printed by Pardy and Son (Printers) Ltd, Ringwood, Hampshire.

Front Cover: The Masons Arms, Branscombe.

INTRODUCTION

Devon is very much a county of contrasts. On the one hand you have busy main roads linking the large towns and cities on the other small villages and hamlets reached down narrow winding lanes. The coastline ranges from large flat sandy bays to steep rugged cliffs whilst the landscape in general varies from green rolling hills and wooded river valleys to harsh open moorland.

During the course of my research I toured the whole county and have combined the best selection of pubs with the most interesting walks. The majority of them are in peaceful village settings and have been chosen purely for their charm or location no charge whatsoever being made for inclusion.

The walks are all circular, vary from 2 miles to 7 miles and are explained in detail each with an accompanying sketch map. They are deliberately short to appeal to all age groups but especially families and although they have been planned to start and finish at the pub one can of course start anywhere along the route happy in the knowledge that refreshment is assured at some point. Parking can sometimes be a tricky problem, and whilst most landlords are very obliging, it is unreasonable to use the car park if you are not visiting the pub. Alternative parking areas are listed but as a matter of course most people seek the landlord's permission first.

The coastal paths are well marked and maintained but many inland routes are in a poor state. Devon County Council is working hard to put the situation right. To help you the reference quoted at the start of each walk refers to the 1:50 000 - $1\frac{1}{4}$ inch to the mile in the Landranger series. The seven maps you would need to cover the whole county are no's 180, 181, 190, 191, 192, 201, and 202. There are more detailed maps in the Pathfinder series they cover an area 1:25 000 - $2\frac{1}{2}$ inches to the mile.

The new "Rights of Way Act" which came into force on August 13th 1990 has much improved the rights of ramblers; it is a massive step forward in path protection. The act now requires occupiers who disturb the land to make good the surface within 24 hours of the disturbance or two weeks if the disturbance is the first one for a particular crop. Where no width is recorded the minimum width of a path must now be one metre and two metres for a bridleway and the exact line of the path must be apparent on the ground. Furthermore the occupier must prevent crops growing on, or encroaching onto the path. If you find a footpath blocked the law allows for you to remove only as much of the obstruction to get by but not to cause damage. If there is no way through you have the right to leave the path and find an alternative route. Any problems you find should be reported to the county engineer in the rights of way section at County Hall in Exeter.

It has been proved that walking is extremely good for you, it is also safe providing a few simple rules are observed. Try to wear suitable clothing. Light weight, waterproof trousers or leggings are advisable as many paths become overgrown in the summer. Strong waterproof boots are best but any comfortable footwear will do provided it is well treaded.

Take care on lanes without pavements and always walk facing the oncoming traffic except on a dangerous right-hand bend. A compass can be useful on open moor land and a torch is handy if walking late in the evening. I always carry a walking stick and find it ideal for clearing nettles and brambles also to test the stability of the ground ahead but most important it can be waived to deter animals.

Wherever you go always remember the country code. Guard against all fires. Fasten gates. Keep dogs under control and always on a lead where there are livestock. Keep to the path across farm land. Take all litter home. Respect wild life and do not pick wild flowers. I very much enjoyed all these walks and the hospitality of the pubs I hope you will too.

Mike Power

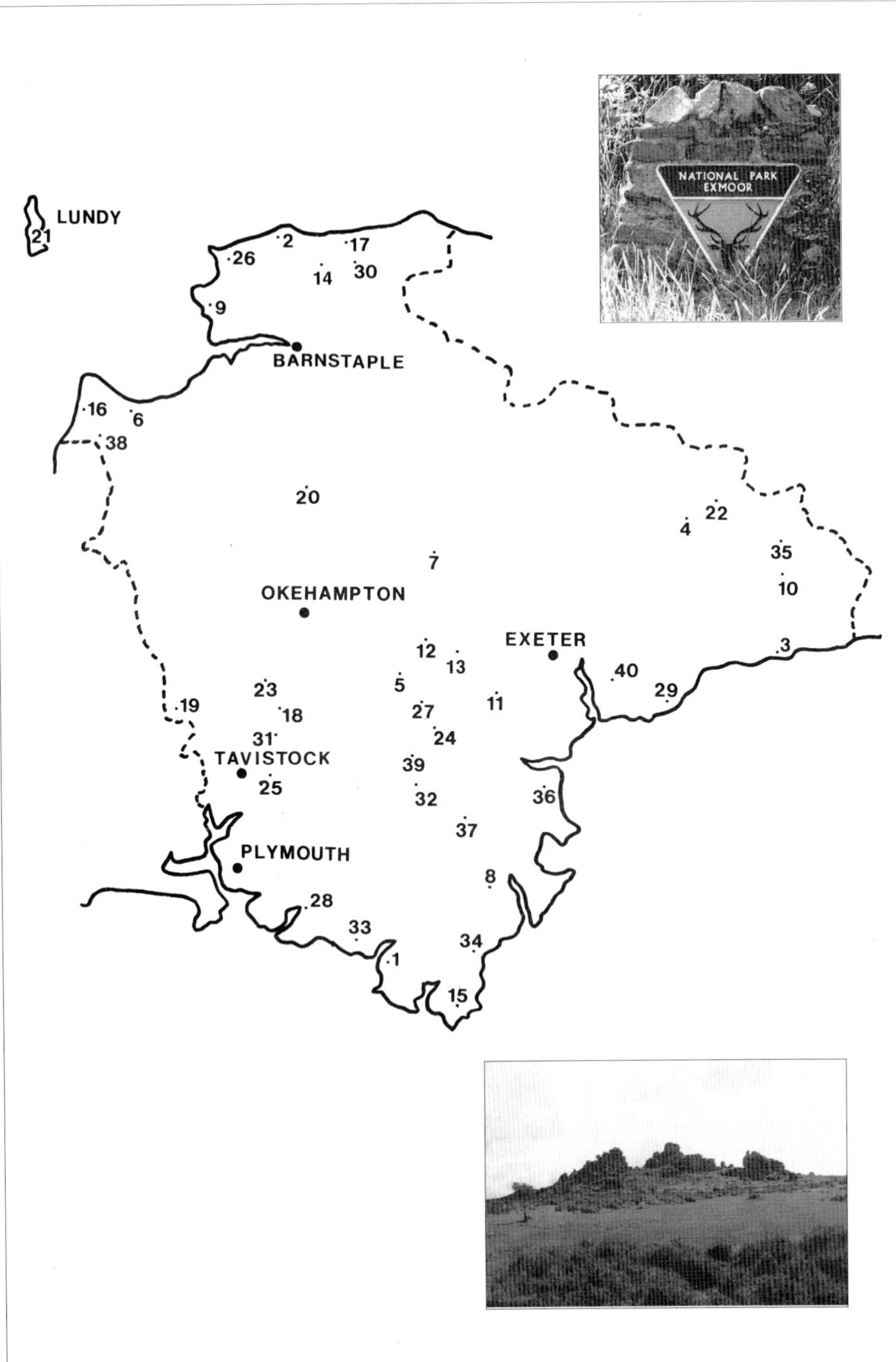

LUNDY
21
26
2
17
14
30
9
BARNSTAPLE
16
6
38
20
22
4
35
7
10
OKEHAMPTON
12
EXETER
13
3
5
40
23
11
29
19
18
27
31
24
TAVISTOCK
39
25
32
36
37
PLYMOUTH
8
28
33
34
1
15
NATIONAL PARK
EXMOOR

The Sloop Inn, Bantham

The Sloop Inn once had associations with smugglers and indeed was at one time owned by John Whiddon, one of the most famous smugglers and wreckers of the South Hams. Built in the 16th century the front bar has a bare stone floor, part wood panelled walls and a timber propped beamed ceiling. The more comfortable, carpeted lounge has warm wood panelling and a large wood burning stove in the stone fireplace. One step takes you into a comfortable dining area beyond which is a family room. Interestingly the bar in these two rooms is built in the shape of a wooden boat.

The inn is a freehouse very well run by the resident owners. The well stocked bar includes an extensive wine list, local cider, bottled beers from around the globe and three real ales, Draught Bass, Ushers Best Bitter and Directors Bitter.

The Sloop has developed a reputation for its very good food with something to suit all tastes. Chalked on the blackboard daily bar snacks include the standard fare of ploughman's and sandwiches plus several speciality salads. "Sloop seafood" is prepared with fresh crab, prawns, smoked salmon, cockles and smoked mackerel. A good choice of seafood starters feature garlic prawns, avocado with crab mousse and samphrie, seafood chowder and crab claws. Lots of fresh fish is available each day. John Dorey is served with an orange sauce while fillets of lemon sole are stuffed with salmon and prawns. There are meat dishes like grilled lamb with Cumberland sauce, braised oxtail and a vegetarian shepherd pie. The line up of tempting homemade sweets includes raspberry pavlova, lemon crunch and traditional spotted dick with custard.

Weekday opening times are from 11 a.m. till 2.30 p.m. and 6 p.m. till 11 p.m. Children are allowed in the dining area and family room and there is no objection to well controlled dogs. Self-catering accommodation is available in three two-bedroom flats at the rear.

Telephone: (0548) 56048934.

Bantham is signed from the A379 between Kingsbridge and Aveton Gifford.

Approx. distance of walk: 2.75 miles. O.S.Map 202 SX 667/437.

Continue along the lane past the pub and park in the Evans Estate car park.

A short but very enjoyable, scenic coastal walk to the village of Thurlestone returning back across farm land. Apart from a couple of steep sections the going is easy and mostly dry underfoot.

From the pub walk down the lane towards the sea, aim left across the car park and pick up the sandy track. Cross the stile into the field on the left and follow the coast path signed, Thurlestone 1 mile. The path is easy to follow. After skirting the golf course a finger post directs you inland. The path rises to meet the fence and leaves by the gate into the lane.

Turn left and make your way up the hill to the church. Bear left and then right onto the gravel track to the left of the church signed, Bantham ½ mile. Further ahead climb the stepped wall and head straight across the field to the stile opposite. After crossing another stile the path heads down the field to a stile in the hedge. From here you get a lovely view of Bantham and beyond to the River Avon. Bearing right walk carefully down the hillside making for the track at the bottom. Cross the stile, and the stream, and immediately go over the crossing point into the field on the left. Bearing slightly right make your way to the stile in the far right-hand hedge and go up the narrow path to the stile at the top following the track back to the pub.

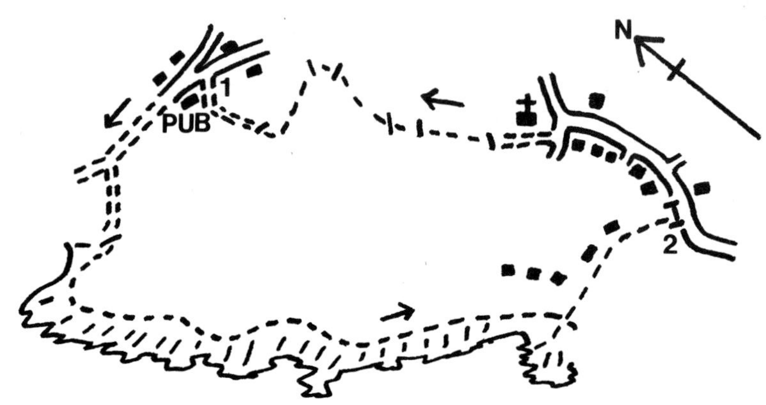

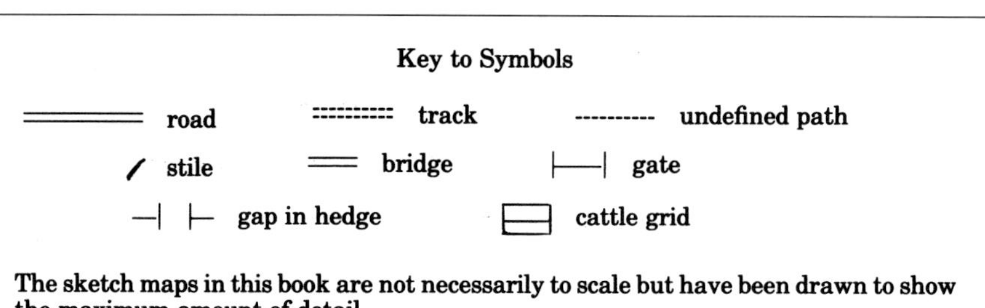

Key to Symbols

═══════ road	·········· track	---------- undefined path
/ stile	══ bridge	⊢—⊣ gate
—⊢ ⊢— gap in hedge	cattle grid	

The sketch maps in this book are not necessarily to scale but have been drawn to show the maximum amount of detail.

Ye Olde Globe, Berrynarbor

Berrynarbor is a lovely village tucked peacefully away in the Sterridge Valley about a mile from the sea. Not surprisingly Berrynarbor was awarded the title of best kept village in 1985 and 1988 and was runner up in 1986, 1989, 1990 and 1991.

The Olde Globe first became a pub in 1675 having been converted from a row of three cottages reputed to date from about 1280, the lime-ash floors alone are over 400 years old. Today one central bar serves three distinct drinking areas. The cosy low beamed front bar has changed little. A tall wooden settle is built into the curved wall beside the large stone fireplace with more settles and tub chairs. The walls, darkened with age, are adorned with many old artifacts and paintings. The equally attractive lounge has an open log fire and diners in the restaurant can enjoy their meal by candlelight. There are picnic tables at the front with more seating in the attractive side garden.

The pub is an Ushers House, now part of Courage, very well run by the friendly tenants, Lynne and Phil Bridle. The well stocked bar includes draught scrumpy, one real ale, Ushers Best Bitter and a good range of wine.

Excellent reasonably priced bar food is available all week with a traditional Sunday roast. Served between 12 noon and 1.15 p.m, the menu offers a range of snacks such as sandwiches, ploughman's, garlic bread, homemade soup, garlic mushrooms, chilli, spaghetti bolognese, lasagne, homemade pizzas, steak and kidney pie, salads and various grills. In the restaurant the choice is more comprehensive. Seven starters are followed by dishes like roast duckling, venison, boeuf bourginon and chicken chasseur with a nut roast Portuguese for vegetarians.

Weekday opening times are from 11 30 a.m. till 2.30. p.m. and 6 p.m. till 11 p.m. Children are welcome in the kitchen bar and the separate family room, dogs too if kept under control.

Telephone: (0271) 882465.

Village is signed from the A399 between Combe Martin and Ilfracombe.

Approx. distance of walk: 3.25 miles O.S.Map 180 SS 560/467.

The car park at the front is very small but there is space in the road behind the pub. Better still use the free car park further up the hill beyond the church.

A very scenic walk along attractive country lanes, through woods and across farm land. Although steep, and wet in a few places, the walk is generally good underfoot.

From the inn turn right, cross the bridge, turn left, then right up Hagginton Hill. After passing under the bridge there is a farm entrance on the left beside which is a permissive path leading into a wood. Take this path, fork right at the junction and follow it as it rises steadily through the trees where you have a lovely view of the village below. It is an attractive path mostly dry underfoot with many wild flowers.

After just over a mile the path bears right into the lane. Turn left walking until you reach a footpath on the left signed, To Sterridge Valley. Climb the stone steps in the wall and bear right, across the field to the stile in the far boundary and continue down in the same direction to meet the stile in the hedge. Cross the bridge and turn left following the path through the trees, over a couple of shallow streams and a stile before entering a field. Walk down beside the hedge to the track then down to the lane and turn left.

It is an attractive walk back as many of the cottage gardens are ablaze with colour with more wild flowers growing in the hedgerows. On the right, near the bottom of the lane there is a signed footpath. Go through the gate, up the field to the stile turning right into the lane at the top and follow it back to the village centre.

The Masons Arms, Branscombe

Branscombe is considered by many to be the prettiest village in East Devon. In 1865 the Manor and most of the parish was bought by H.Ford, Esquire, whose family preserved the unspoilt beauty of the village, a large part of which is now owned by The National Trust. Pretty stone cottages cling to the sides of the surrounding narrow lanes with more attractive stone and thatched cottages in the village itself.

In the centre is the charming Branscombe Arms. Built in the fourteenth century, and once a favourite haunt for smugglers, this pretty vine covered inn lies beside a small stream half a mile from the sea. Today it is run both as an hotel and a pub a combination which works well. The pub, although not totally original, has a lovely old world charm with white painted stone walls and a low beamed ceiling. Still preserved is the old flag stone floor between the bar and the massive inglenook fireplace where, every Thursday lunchtime, a joint is roasted over the log fire. Comfortable seating is neatly arranged on the attractive front terrace. A walkers guide to Branscombe Village, which is on sale in the bar, has a photograph showing how the inn looked in the 1900's.

The Masons Arms is a free house presently serving three real ales Wadworth 6X, Draught Bass and Dartmoor Best.

An excellent bar menu, served from 7 p.m. and supplemented by daily specials, includes soup of the day followed by moules marinieres, grilled whole lemon sole, homemade duck and bacon pie, steamed steak and kidney pudding, pan fried lamb cutlets, tagliatelle with a pesto and ham sauce and a cold chicken salad. Tempting sweets range from apple strudel to creme brulee.

Weekday opening times are from 11 a.m. till 2.30 p.m. (3 p.m. on Saturday) and 5.30 p.m. till 11 p.m. Excellent accommodation is available throughout the year. Children are not allowed in the bar.

Telephone: (029780) 300.

Branscombe is signed from the 3052 between Sidmouth and Seaton.

Approx. distance of walk: 4.25 miles O.S.Map 192 SY 204/888.

There is a car park behind the pub but because the lanes are narrow the only suitable alternative is in the road to the beach opposite.

Branscombe is a very picturesque village nestling in a peaceful valley close to the sea. This lovely scenic walk, demanding in places and often muddy, at first heads inland through attractive woodland, follows a stream then crosses farm land onto a bridleway before joining with the South Devon Coast Path. After reaching the valley the path heads back to the village beside a stream.

Turn left from the pub climbing the hill towards Seaton. Look for the lane on the left signed to Lower House. Walk down past the dwellings and ford the stream into the lane at the bottom. Turn left, and in a couple of hundred yards look for the signed footpath on the right. Pass through the farm gates and go up the narrow grass track turning right through the small gate onto the signed path leading up into the field.

Keep straight ahead in the direction of the finger post towards the stile beside the gate. Turn right and walk to the stile in the corner of the field then turn right keeping close to the hedge. Turn left at the finger post, cross the field to the stile then bear right down the hillside to the gate, out into the lane and turn left.

After walking for some distance, and almost opposite the entrance to Barnel, go through the gap into the field on the right and bear right down the bank to pick up the muddy footpath close to the stream. Eventually a small bridge allows access to the opposite bank. Bear right gradually walking away from the stream up the rise. After passing the house in the valley go out through the farm gate into the lane and turn left.

Walk up past Hole House and turn left. In a couple of hundred yards take the signed bridleway on the right up through the woods, out onto the drive at the top and turn left. Pass through the gate and turn right onto the stoney track. When you reach the open grass area bear right up to the farm

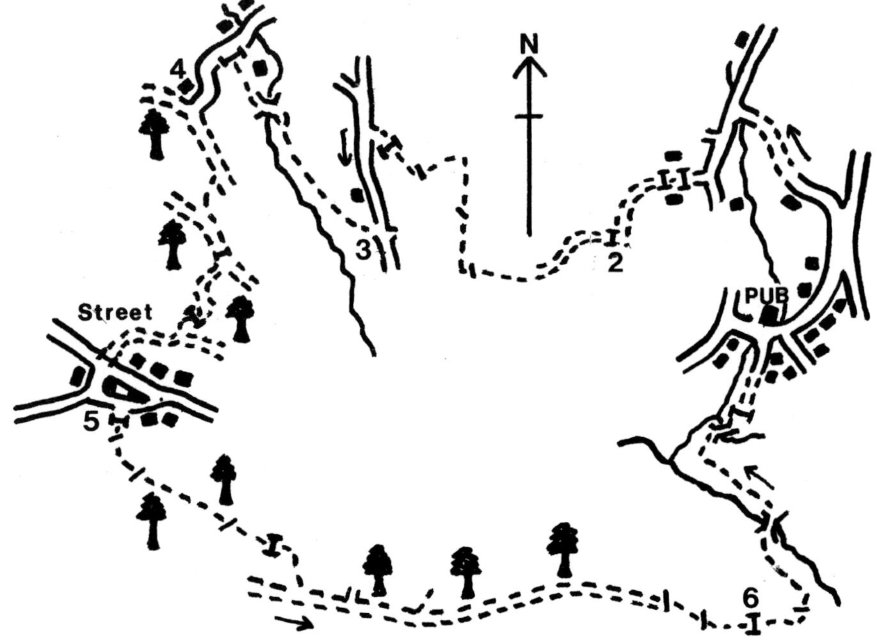

gate and into the field. Keep straight ahead down the field to join with the track, turn right, pass through the gate and continue down to the gate at the bottom. The Fountain Head is a very good half way refreshment stop.

Pass in front of the pub, turn left into the lane and almost immediately take the signed footpath on the right. Go through the gate, over the stile into the field and follow the path up to the stile and into Pitt Coppice. At the top cross the stile into the field, walk over to the gate, pass through and bear right to join with the South Devon Coast Path.

Ignoring the side paths follow the track to the cliff top and head down to Branscombe Mouth.

As you near the bottom pass through the kissing gate, through the gap in the wire fence and walk down to the stile. Turn left following the path beside the stream until a gate allows access to the small bridge. Continue following the path, through a small gate then through a wide farm gate beside a stream and turn right. Cross the stream, pass through the gate and proceed up the stone track back to the pub.

The Fountain Head, Street

Broadhembury

Drewe Arms, Broadhembury

Broadhembury is one of the most attractive villages in Devon. The lovely Drewe Arms, like all the other cottages that flank the main street of this picture post card village, is thatched and painted white. Dominated by an enormous open fireplace the main seating area is separated from the bar by a high back wooden settle. The room has a beamed ceiling with lots of old tools and other implements adorning the part panelled walls and displayed on the high mantelpiece. There is an interesting assortment of furniture including a church pew running the entire length of one wall in the smaller bar. A separate "Tea Room" is laid out for dining and there are picnic benches on the lawn.

The inn is a freehouse very well run by the owners, Kerstin and Nigel Burge. Real ale is still dispensed traditionally straight from barrels built into an old wooden cabinet. The list usually includes Dartmoor Bitter, Cotleigh Tawny Bitter and Draught Bass.

An excellent menu is available seven days a week except Sunday evening. On a recent visit the blackboard offered tasty tomato and basil soup plus an interesting choice of open sandwiches. "Gang plank" is made with rare beef, gravad lax, Brie and prawns. Although mostly fish such as fresh mussels in garlic butter, fresh griddled sardines and dressed crab the list did include fillet of beef served with green peppercorn sauce and Blackdown venison with field mushrooms. In addition the three course set menu offered a choice of nine starters. There were fresh scallops holandaise or pickled herring served with a glass of Aquavit followed by fresh turbot, fillet of halibut with anchovy butter, monkfish and grilled red mullet.

The pub is open all day in the summer from 11 a.m. till 11 p.m but closed between 2.30 p.m. and 6 p.m. in the winter. Well behaved children are welcome.

Telephone: (040484) 267.

Walk No. 4

The village is signed 1 mile from the A373 between Honiton and Cullompton.

Approx. distance of walk: 4.75 miles. O.S.Map 192 ST 102/048.

Park at the pub or in the village street.

An enjoyable scenic walk which although hilly is not over demanding. The first half is on peaceful country lanes then along a bridleway beside woods. After passing through the grounds of the local flying club the path enters a bluebell wood before crossing farm land back to the pub.

Take the road on the right out of the village, bear left at the road junction then right at the T junction towards Dunkeswell. The lane rises steadily for some distance snaking its way fairly steeply up through two wooded areas before reaching a signed bridleway near the top on the left.

Bluebells have spread from the woods and carpet the path in early summer. Pass through the gates and continue straight ahead across the field to pick up the short track leading to a farm gate. Walk on, through one last gate then bear right following the track up to the lane and turn left.

In two hundred yards turn left into the entrance to the Devon and Somerset Flying Club, walk up to the gate, enter the airfield and turn left. Keeping to the main track walk round past the buildings and mobile homes then across the grass, walking fairly close to the boundary on the left until you reach a gateway which allows access to the signed bridleway. Follow the track down to the gate and into the bluebell wood.

After a while you will come to a new stile in the hedge on the left, cross into the field and bear right over to the stile in the far hedge. Follow the path through the small wood to the stile then walk down the field to the bottom. A stile beside the gates leads on to a short track emerging into a field. Walk straight ahead to the stile then bear right crossing the brook to one last stile in the far hedge. Turn right into the lane and then left over the bridge back to the village centre.

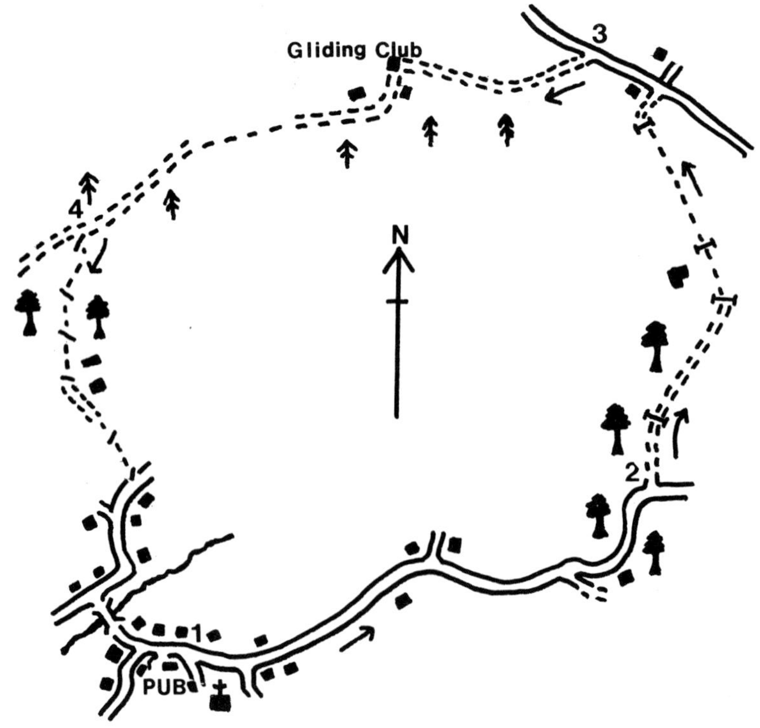

Bullers Arms, Chagford

Once quiet and sleepy today Chagford is a bustling Dartmoor village very well served with pubs having no less than four in the same street. The Bullers Arms is a genuine village local, and although originally an old coaching inn, the Victorian front was only added after a disastrous fire destroyed it and most of the other properties in the street.

Named after a local soldier from Credition, the simply furnished front bar has lots of military badges decorating the part wood panelled walls. There is also more seating in the original area of the pub which still has bulging white painted walls behind which is a separate cosy restaurant. A door leads out on to the sunny back terrace, attractively decorated with flowers and where barbecues are held in summer.

The inn is a free house very well run by the friendly owners, Bob Lewis-Jones and Keith Wright. Two well kept, prize winning real ales are served by handpump, Dartmoor Best and Burton Ale. Coffee is also available by the cup and tea by the pot.

The bar menu, chalked on the blackboard and ordered from a separate servery, offers ploughman's, Devon pasties and soup. Among the starters, listed are crispy white bait and tiger prawns and to follow a choice of fish, steak and kidney pudding and various steaks. Specials might include fish pie and home cooked beef and pineapple served with potatoes and stir fried vegetables. Vegetarians can choose from daily specials such as mushroom stroganoff, vegetable pie, cauliflower cheese and harvest pie made with filo pastry. To complete your meal there are tempting sweets like raspberry cheese cake with clotted cream. Children are not forgotten having their own menu.

Weekday opening times are from 11 a.m. till 2.30/3 p.m. and 6 p.m. till 11 p.m. Dogs are welcome if kept on a lead.

Telephone: (0647) 432348.

Chagford is signed west from the A382 about three miles north west from Moretonhampstead.

Approx. distance of walk: 4 miles. O.S.Map 191 SX 697/877.

Park where you can in the village.

An enjoyable walk partly along peaceful country lanes and on very attractive footpaths especially the river walk along the banks of the Teign. The only tricky section can be the stepping stones across the Teign as they are widely spaced and partially covered with water when the river level is high.

From the Bullers Arms turn left and walk to the end of the street, go past the church into the lane on the left and immediately take the turning on the left signed, Great Weeke and Yellam. Further down turn left into Adley Lane walking as far as the signed footpath on the left. Go up the track to the stile, over into the field and bear right across to the stile in the far hedge. Continue in the same direction, over one more stile and follow the little path out into the cul-de-sac, up to the road and turn left.

In fifty yards go over the stile and cut across the field to Rushford Bridge. Cross the bridge and climb over the stile into the field on the left making your way to the corner of the field. Pass through the gap in the hedge on the right and bear left across to the small bridge. From here the path is well signed and easy to follow running for the most part beside the river. It is a delightful footpath which at one point passes though a small attractive wood. Eventually after a series of stiles and gates you reach the lane.

Turn right and in twenty steps take the footpath on the left signed, to Murchington. It is a very pretty path climbing steadily up through the trees. Attractive moss covered stones and lots of wild flowers line the route. Keep following the path until the finger post directs you left across stepping stones to a stile. Following a line fairly close to the hedge on the left head up the field to the stile turning left into the lane at the top.

Keep left at the road junction, through Murchington and further on, as the road descends, look for the signed bridleway on the left. Follow the track down until you reach the gate but do not enter the National Trust property take the narrow gully on the right down to the river. Carefully cross by the stepping stones to pick up the track on the far side, follow it up to the lane and turn left. Extremely picturesque the lane follows the river passing Holystreet Manor. Keep straight ahead at the road junction and climb the lane back up to the village.

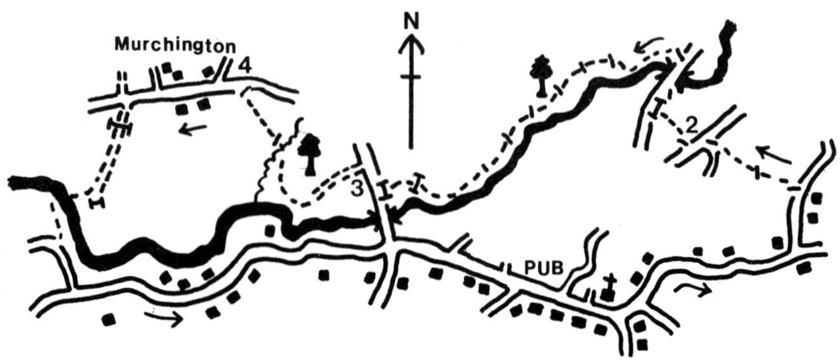

The sketch maps in this book are not necessarily to scale but have been drawn to show the maximum amount of detail.

The footpath beside the Teign, Chagford

Clovelly

Red Lion Hotel, Clovelly

Picturesque Clovelly is probably the most visited village in Devon but to see it at its best be there early in the morning or after 6 p.m. when most of the day trippers have left. Apart from the enormous visitor centre, which is completely out of character, time has stood still. George Carey had the village built about 400 years ago after diverting a stream. Cobbles were laid on the bed which still remain today. Despite the many visitors life carries on as normal in what is still very much a working village. Goods are hauled down on wooden sledges, work originally done by donkeys but now mostly used to convey holiday makers.

Few pubs can boast a more enviable position than The Red Lion. Located on the harbour front the main bar overlooks the quay so too does the restaurant immediately above. The old, original back bar, the one the locals use, is mellow with age, comfortably furnished and has bare stone walls, a beamed ceiling and heated in winter by a warm open fire. On fine sunny days people spill out onto the harbour wall to enjoy their drinks whilst taking in the lovely sea air.

The Red Lion is a freehouse presently offering two real ales Wadworth 6X and Burton Ale.

A limited choice of very good bar food is chalked daily on the blackboard. Dishes such as oysters, fresh mussels cooked in wine, baked potatoes, curry and tasty fisherman's soup served with garlic croutons and grated cheese. Diners in the restaurant can select from an imaginative menu offering meals like smoked goose and nut salad or a brace of quails in port sauce. Fresh fish naturally features on the menu with local crab and lobster in prominence and there are always at least two vegetarian dishes.

The inn opens early serving coffee from 10 a.m. and lunch from 11.30 a.m. Families are welcome and dogs on a lead in the bar. Comfortable accommodation is provided in 12 en-suite rooms.

Telephone: (0237) 431 237.

The village is signed from the A39 west from Barnstaple at Clovelly Cross.

Approx. distance of walk: 4 miles. O.S.Map 190 SS 318/248.

As parking is very limited you are recommended to use the main car park signed on the approach to the village. Access to Clovelly is through the large terminal type building, where the parking charge is collected, or from the approach road.

To reach the pub and see the village the only way down is the traffic free cobbled street. You can walk or take a donkey any day except Friday when they have their day off. To just visit the pub a regular Land Rover taxi service uses the lane at the back but usually stops by 5.30.p.m. The walk is very scenic which first takes you through bluebell woods and along the cliff top coast path than inland up a river valley before returning to the village across farm land. Whilst not over demanding some sections are steep and there are a few wet areas.

Pass through the arch to the back of the pub and walk to the top of the lane. Just before reaching the road turn right through the green gate onto the signed coast path. Follow the well worn track to the right, forking right at the finger post. Further ahead pass through the kissing gate into the field walking beside the fence until directed through a small wooden gate on to an attractive hillside path. After re-entering the field turn right, pass through the gate into the bluebell wood, bear right at the track and then fork right. When you rejoin the track bear right keeping to the coast path which eventually dips steeply down through trees to meet another track. Turn left and then right.

As you approach the shore you have a lovely view of Lundy Island. Turn left down the gully, cross the stream and head inland on the signed path past the old lime kiln. Ignore the signed path on the right but continue ahead following the narrow track as it rises steadily through an attractive lush valley. Turn left at the bridleway over the bridge then left again at the track.

In two hundred paces a fingerpost on the right directs you onto a bridlepath up a steep, stoney gully. Pass through the gate into the field and keep straight ahead towards the finger post. Go through the gate into the field, turn right and then left at the top along the hedge boundary. Leave by the gate on the far side keeping straight ahead to the gate, through the farm yard and into the lane. Continue past the church of "All Saints", worth a visit for its ancient font and Norman porch, and leave by the main entrance turning left into the road back down to the village.

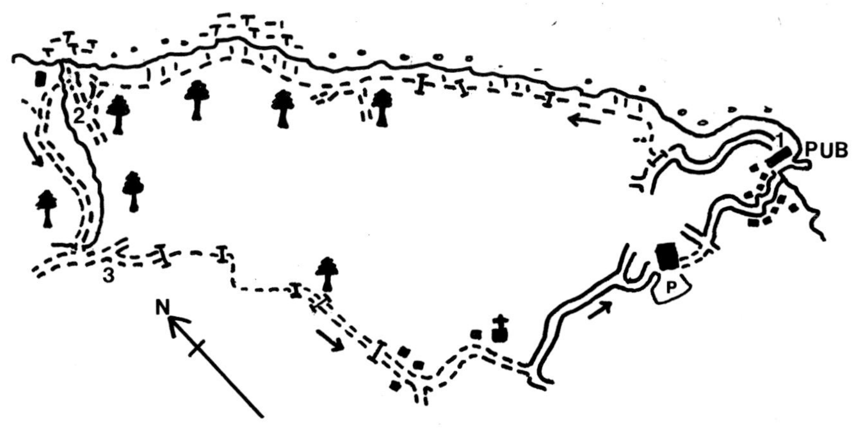

New Inn, Coleford

Popular with diners this ancient thatched coaching Inn nestles beside a stream in the pretty Devon, farming village of Coleford. Much of the 13th century building still remains. Bare stone walls, wooden settles and a low beamed ceiling are features of the front bar whilst the similar side bar has padded settles and a friendly resident parrot named Captain. On cold winter days you can sit by one of the open log fires, and in fine weather beside the stream in the attractive courtyard and garden.

The inn is a freehouse beautifully kept and personally run by the friendly owners, Paul and Irene Butt. There are four real ales on hand pump, three regulars, Wadworth 6X, Flowers I.P.A. and Flowers Original plus a guest beer.

An imaginative food menu, served seven days a week in the bar or in the beautiful stone floored dining area, is cooked to order useing fresh local produce wherever possible. Heading the list on the blackboard are Ploughman's made with local cheese and cream of pea and ham soup followed by slices of pork fillet in a cream, mushroom and sherry sauce, lamb in a creamy rosemary sauce and tandoori chicken. There is Turkish lamb with herb rice, natural oak smoked haddock, mussels in cider, beef curry and spaghetti bolognese. You might prefer to choose a seasonal salad such as smoked trout with a gooseberry sauce or nicoise with tuna, olives and eggs. Vegetarians can enjoy ratatouille with a cheese topping, taglitelle with mushrooms and Stilton or cauliflower and cashew nut mornay. Tempting sweets might include caramel nectarines with caramel ice cream and cream.

Opening times in the week are from 11.30 a.m. till 2.30 p.m. and 6 p.m. till 11 p.m. Whilst children are not allowed in the bar they are welcome in the dining area. Dogs are allowed in the bar but must be kept on a lead. Bed and breakfast is available in self catering accommodation.

Telephone: (0363) 84242.

Coleford is a remote farming hamlet 3 miles west of Crediton best reached south from the A3072 at Copplestone.

Approx. distance of walk: 4 miles O.S.Map. 191 SS 773/012.

Although the inn has its own large car park there is some limited parking outside in the lane.

Footpaths are few in the area around Coleford and most are in poor condition a situation which will hopefully be put right soon. This scenic walk is across farm land and along peaceful country lanes.

From the New Inn car park turn left, and in a short way, go through the metal gate on the left adjacent to a road sign for Coleford. Make your way across the field to the railway underpass. Shortly afterwards climb a stile into some bushes following the path as best you can to reach a second stile. Walk along the edge of the field keeping to the hedge on the left until you reach a stile beside the gate in the corner. Cross into the field and continue with the hedge on your right, up to the stile and out into Knowle Lane.

Proceed along this very pleasant country lane passing Tapps Farm and through the small hamlet of Knowle. Look for a sign on the right, "Unsuitable for Motors" and turn onto this gravel track. Turn right when you reach the road at Harland Cross and steadily climb up to the crossroads at the top of the hill. Carefully cross over and continue ahead, past the refuse tip on your left. This section is the only one where you may encounter some traffic and as there are no pavements care should be taken. Walk down the hill and look for a gateway on your right, marked "South Coombe".

Pass through the gate and proceed down to the buildings at South Coombe, through a second gate and then a third to the left of a large oak. Cross the stream and climb the fence into a meadow. At the time of writing there were no waymarks and some ground work was necessary to establish the route - hopefully this situation has now been remedied. Proceed along the valley, keeping the hedge on your right, through several gates, always keeping the hedge to your right, until Penstone is sighted.

The path then bears right between farm buildings and enters the lane. Walk straight up the road to the village, turning left under the railway bridge and then over the river bridge. Turn right at the T junction, cross the bridge, and when you reach the crossroads at Coleford turn right back to the pub.

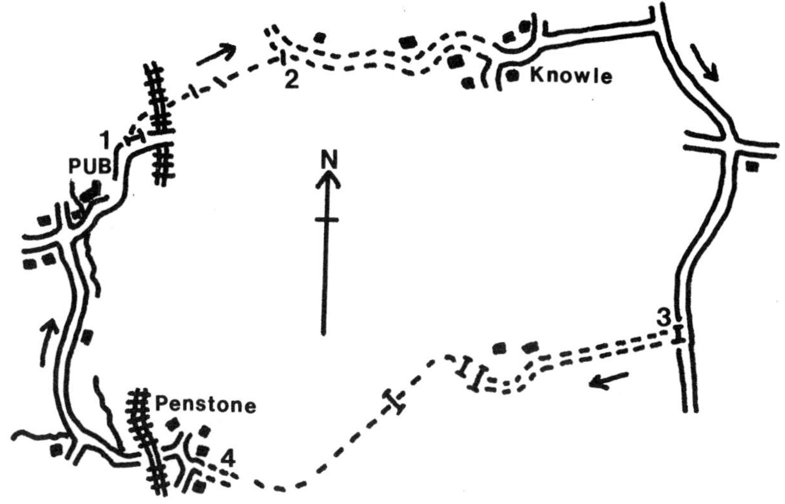

Hunters Lodge Inn, Cornworthy

Cornworthy is a small village in a very attractive part of South Hams especially the area to the north where the River Harbourne flows through Bow Creek to the Dart. Although the area generally is well served with pubs few compare with the Hunters Lodge Inn.

It is a delightful pub beautifully kept and very well run by the friendly owners Rob and Deb. The two rooms of the main bar have low beamed ceilings, bare brick walls with pew style bench seating and captain's chairs. The adjoining cosy dining room is similar in appearance but has a warm log fire in the large stone fireplace. The tables are beautifully set with very pretty blue table linen.

The inn is a freehouse serving two real ales Ushers Best and 44 Special - a mid brown malty beer from Blackawton the oldest brewery in Devon.

The food at the Hunters Inn is quite remarkable even by restaurant standards and booking is essential at weekends. Predominantly fish all meals are prepared from fresh local produce and lovingly cooked by Deb. Except Sunday lunch time when there is a traditional roast, tempting bar snack include tasty homemade soup, cottage pie, sweet and sour crispy cod and chicken Maryland. From the large list of starters you can indulge in deep fried mussels with garlic, squid rings, grilled jumbo sardines, baked stuffed mushrooms, homemade gravad lax and scallops sauted with mushrooms, smoked bacon and onion in wine with cream and herbs. Main meals might include pork fillet fried with capers, half a roast duck in a Cointreau and wine sauce, chicken breast with lobster and prawns in herbs topped with hollandaise, beef Wellington and pan fried venison steaks. A popular fish dish is halibut in lime and wine with prawns and crab claws also for lovers of seafood, half a grilled lobster thermidor, seafood mixed grill and a whole cracked crab.

Weekday opening times are from 11.30 a.m. till 3 p.m. and 6.30 p.m. till 11 p.m. Children are welcome and dogs too in the bar on a lead.

Telephone: (0803) 732 204.

Cornworthy is signed from the A381 south of Totnes.

Approx. distance of walk: 2.5 miles. O.S.Map 202 SX 827/556.

Park in the main village street.

An extremely enjoyable scenic walk down to Bow Creek, then along a pretty path beside the river to the picturesque hamlet of Tuckenhay. The route back to the pub is along a narrow leafy track. It is an ideal walk for a sunny Sunday morning, fairly short, not too demanding and mostly dry underfoot.

Turn left from the pub and walk up the hill. Just beyond the cul-de-sac turn left into the entrance to Cornworthy Court walking through the farm yard onto the track at the back. In three hundred yards fork left and continue down the track to the gate. Pass through into the field keeping straight ahead down to the waters edge and turn left.

Follow the shore line crossing the stile and further ahead bear left as the path rises up through the trees and enters a field. Leave by the stile and continue along the path into the meadow and back down to the edge of the creek. Cross the stream and head away from the river through the gate onto the track. Immediately bear right and continue along the path which rises up to join a larger path. Further ahead cross the stile walking round the field to a second stile and onto a pretty path which eventually brings you out into the lane at Tuckenhay.

If you want to visit The Malsters Arms (owned by Keith Floyd the television chef) turn right cross, the bridge then right again otherwise turn left on to the stoney track. Part way up climb the steps to the stile leading into the field and aim for the stile in the top left-hand corner taking time to look back over your shoulder at Tuckenhay below. Follow the track until you eventually reach the village then keep straight ahead into the lane and turn left back to the pub.

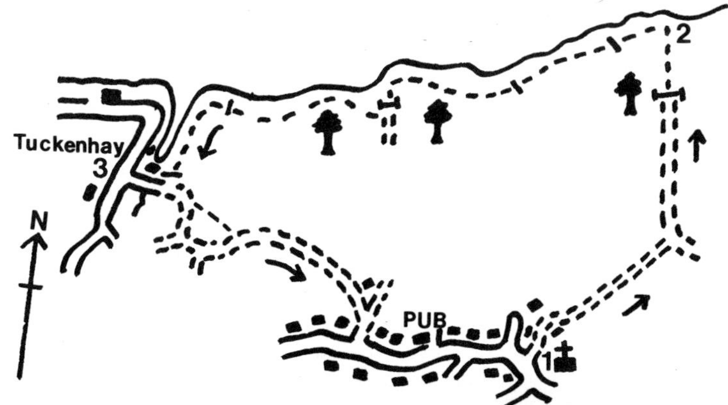

The Thatched Barn Inn, Croyde

Croyde was the landing-place of the Viking Chief named Crida from whom the village takes its name. Rollers from the Atlantic crash on to the vast expanse of open sands making It an ideal holiday location for the many surfers who crowd its streets and shops throughout the season and find refreshment in the attractive Thatched Barn Inn.

"The Thatch" as it was known locally, dates back to the 14th century and was used for the storage of farm animals and the brewing of beer for the monks of the nearby, ancient St Helen's Priory. It was not until 1978 that it was converted into the present pub. Although extensive alterations have taken place much of the original building is still preserved. The bars have heavily beamed ceilings and white painted walls with wooden settles and window seats. There is a large attractive restaurant behind a smaller dining area and tables and chairs on the sunny front terrace.

The inn is a freehouse very well run by the owners son Rocky. Coffee is served from 10 a.m, after which you have the choice of three real ales, Burton Ale, Tetley Bitter plus a guest ale.

Food starts early with a choice of full English or vegetarian breakfast followed by lunchtime bar snacks such as homemade soup, sandwiches, jacket potatoes, generous ploughman's and various salads. The main menu lists lentil and hazelnut pate and "nachos" - tortilla chips with cheese, peppers, chilli and sour cream also homemade lasagne, freshly baked fish pie and curry. There is usually a good choice of fish like Dover sole and lobster and house specials which include Exmoor venison and "Thatch" special ribs. Vegetarians can choose from several dishes on the set menu plus more chalked daily on the blackboard.

During the week, from Whitsun through till September, the inn is open all day but closed for the rest of the year between 3 p.m. and 7 p.m. Families are welcome. Accommodation is available.

Telephone: (0271) 890349.

Croyde, a popular village for surfers, is signed west from the A361 between Ilfracombe and Barnstaple.

Approx. distance of walk: 3.25 miles. O.S.Map 180 SS 444/392.

The pub has its own car park opposite but there are several parking places in the road at the front.

A most enjoyable, scenic coastal walk which first crosses Croyde Bay on the Somerset and North Devon Coast Path and then heads up on to Saunton Down with breathtaking views across Saunton Sands. Although steep in places it is not over demanding making it ideal for all the family.

Turn left from the inn then left again onto the path which runs down beside The Carpenter's Arms signed, To The Sands. When you reach the grass continue ahead then bear right to pick up the path down to the shore and turn left. Walking is much easier on the firm damp sand close to the waters edge. On the far side ignore the steps up the cliff but follow the signed path round the rocks on the right, then climb the steps to the gate on the right and follow the signed coast path along the cliff edge. Beyond the next gate the path is signed up the cliff to the road.

Turn left, and in 100 yards, climb the steps on the right to rejoin the coast path. Take the path that runs beside the road not the stepped path up the down. It is very good underfoot and there are lovely views across Saunton Sands. After about a mile the path joins with another from the road. Turn left here, cross the stile and head up the path which rises quite steeply to the field at the top.

Bear left past the derelict cottages up to the finger post in the wall at the top. Walk across the field to the stile in the wall and continue ahead to the stiles in the far fence. Go over into the field and bear right following the well trodden path down to the stile which leads to the shaded path between the fields. At the bottom go over the stile on the left following the signed path to Croyde. Cross the stile into the lane back round to the village. In early summer the walls are covered with masses of pink, white and red Valerian - a lovely sight.

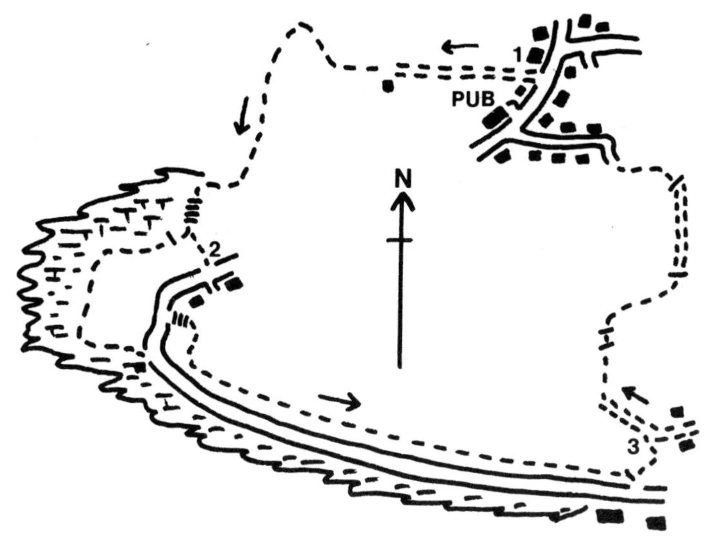

The Tuckers Arms, Dalwood

The attractive, thatched Tuckers Arms is situated in the centre of Dalwood close to the brook. It is a very old country inn dating back to the 13th century - much of which is still original. In summer the front is prettily decked with many colourful hanging baskets and tubs.

From the narrow flagstoned corridor one enters directly into the main bar. The low ceilings are part boarded, plastered and beamed. In winter there is a welcoming log fire in the lovely old inglenook fireplace. Seating is an assortment of padded window seats and wooden settles. There are two partitioned dining areas, a separate public bar where a large collection of miniatures are displayed in cases around the walls, a large function room/skittle alley and a small sunny terrace.

The inn is a freehouse well run by the owners, Kate and David Beck. Real ales presently available include Draught Bass, Boddingtons Bitter and Wadworth 6X.

Good home cooked food is served seven days a week with a traditional Sunday lunch. Apart from ploughman's and sandwiches the bar menu offers homemade soup and a choice of meat platters. Their own homemade curry and lasagne are both very popular so too are the pub's specialities. "Tuckers" skins come with a choice of dips like Stilton and port, "Tuckers Tidies" are pillars of light puff pastry with a choice of homemade fillings, "Trawlerman's" is a mixture of seafood with mushrooms in a white wine and cream sauce and "Springtime" is tender slices of lamb in a casserole of sweet peppers and fresh ginger. Other specialities are pan fried pork schnitzel with lemon and breast of duck sauted in butter with fresh herbs, field mushrooms and bacon served with a rich juniper berry and port wine sauce. Vegetarians are well catered for as are children who have their own menu.

Weekday opening times are from 11.30 a.m. till 3 p.m. and 6.30 p.m. till 11 p.m. Overnight accommodation is available in en-suite rooms.

Telephone: (040488) 342.

Dalwood is signed at several places from the A35 between Honiton and Axminster.

Approx. distance of walk: 5 miles. O.S.Map 192 ST 248/005.

Park anywhere in the lane at the front.

A very enjoyable and varied walk which first crosses open farm land and then follows and crosses the River Yarty. The route back is on bridleways and along peaceful country lanes passing through Heathstock. In places the walk can be quite steep and often muddy making the going a little demanding.

From the inn turn right, cross the river and keep straight ahead on to the concrete farm road to the right of the telephone kiosk. Pass through the gate and head up the field making for the wooden crossing point in the corner. Walk straight ahead to the gap in the hedge, bear right and follow the path up onto the drive to the house, out into the lane and turn left.

Turn right at the crossroads walking to the end of the lane. After passing the house, and a short distance along the grass track, go immediately left through the gate and head down the field in the direction of the finger post. Climb the stile in the far hedge and continue down to the gate at the bottom, bear left up to the lane and keep straight ahead on the road to Membury.

After crossing the River Yarty go through the gate into the field on the left and follow the path close to the river until it bears right beside the hedge and you reach a small gate leading into an area of scrub. Follow the path ahead up to a wooden crossing point then proceed across the field to the gate, out into the lane and keep straight ahead up to the farm.

Ignore the track on the left and the short track straight ahead up to the farm buildings but take the footpath on the right up through the trees. Take care as running water has carved a gully making the surface rather uneven and difficult to climb. At the top cross the farm road and keep straight ahead on to the track. Pass through the farm gate, cross the field and leave by the gate on the far side. Continue along the gravel road then take the turning on the left down to the ford. If the water is too deep cross over on the two small bridges reached through the hedge on the left. Walk up to the lane and turn right.

Turn left just before the bend and fork right onto the bridleway. Bear right at the top following the wider track uphill and then down bearing left, between the dwellings, turning right into the lane at Heathstock.

Turn left at the T junction and walk down towards Lower Corry. It is a very attractive and peaceful lane with many wild flowers growing in the hedgerows. After about a mile, and just before passing under the power lines, you will see there is a gate on the right almost opposite a house. Go through and bear left, behind the farm buildings, down to the brook. Keeping close to the edge follow the path, over a couple of wooden crossing points and a stile until you reach the bridge then cross to the opposite bank and turn left. Finally cross the bridge beside the hedge, go out through the gate into the lane and turn right back to the pub.

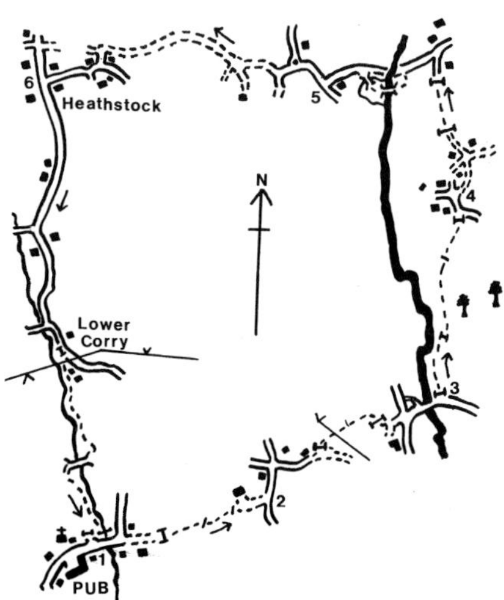

The Nobody Inn, Doddiscombsleigh

Glowing reports are constantly written about this lovely pub and justifiably so. Although the building is ancient the first recording of an inn was not until 1838 when William Diggines inherited the building. The cosy old world interior has a low beamed ceiling with a lovely old inglenook stone fireplace in the main bar. There is a separate, equally attractive restaurant and a small sunny terrace with lovely views of the surrounding hills.

The inn is a free house extremely well run by the owners. Never have I seen a better stocked bar. Real ale is served by hand from The Exe Valley Brewery, Draught Bass and Flowers I.P.A. Listed on the wall of the bar are 200 or more whiskeys but the "piece de resistance" is the wine list with no less then 700 to choose from accompanied by tasting notes.

Bar food is reasonably priced with a vegetarian emphasis . "Nobodys soup" is a unique homemade soup with lots of goodies and based on chicken stock. Almost any sandwich can be made to order plus the ultimate toasted sandwich. An individual mutton pie is served with tatties and neaps. Also listed are macaroni cheese, butter bean casserole, nut roast and hot harvest pie, plus a daily special such as game pie. Two tempting homemade sweets are spiced bread pudding and warm treacle tart with clotted cream. From Wednesday to Saturday a more comprehensive menu is served in the restaurant. One of two specialities, which usually require a days notice, is a large trout stuffed with a delicious mixture of herb butter, sultanas and asparagus and cooked in a very fine pastry. A large list of local produce to takeaway includes local Devon cheese, honey and clotted cream.

Weekday opening times are from 12 noon till 2.30 p.m. and 6 p.m.(7 p.m. in the winter) till 11 p.m No dogs and Children in the restaurant only. Accommodation is available.

Telephone: (0647) 52394.

The village is just to the east of The Dartmoor National Park signed from the B3193 north from the A38.

Approx. distance of walk: 4 miles. O.S.Map 191 SX 855/866.

There is a fair sized car park behind the inn but only limited parking in the lane outside.

An enjoyable walk along peaceful country lanes, on a bridleway, across farm land and on a public footpath through woods. Although hilly in places it is not too demanding but can be a little muddy in bad weather.

Leave the inn turning right and after passing the parish church of St Michael turn left into the lane. Walk straight across at the road junction onto the signed bridleway. It is an attractive path, steeply banked in places and often very muddy. Pass through the gate into the field, and keeping fairly close to the hedge on the left, walk up to the gate at the top turning left into the lane.

Keep left at the junction and after about a mile take the signed footpath on the left. Walk up the drive towards the farm house then bear left taking the narrow path on the left of the house, up to the gate, out onto the track and turn right. When you reach the barn go into the field on the right and walk down beside the field boundary to rejoin the track. At the end go into the field on the left and, keeping close to the hedge on the right, walk down to the stile and enter the woods. The path is a little difficult to follow made worse by fallen trees. It meanders its way fairly close to the field boundary on the right. Eventually you will reach a path junction close to a large tree. Take the path off to the right which leads up to a stile.

Go over into the field and walk down to the bridge and stile, cross into the meadow and bear left. Further on follow the signed path on the right through the scrub up to the stile at the top. There are many wild flowers growing along the path, Primroses, Wood Anemones, purple Orchids, Violets and Bluebells to name but a few. Cross the lane into the drive opposite and follow it down bearing left on to the track opposite the drive to the house. Pass through the gate and immediately go over the stile into the field on the left. Walk straight ahead to the stile in the fence then across to the pair of stiles in the far hedge and bear right, up the field in the direction the church. Leave by the gate at the top and turn right back to the pub.

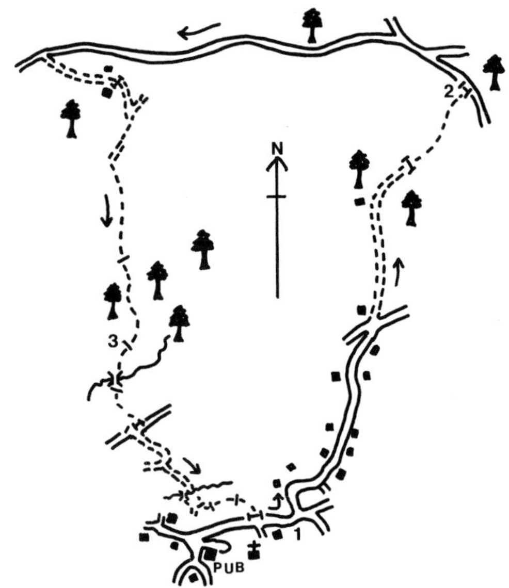

Drewe Arms, Drewsteignton

Drewsteignton is a lovely Devon village and although visited by many tourists each year, happily still remains un-spoilt. The earliest evidence of man in the region is Spinster's Rock - the remains of a Neolithic burial chamber. The population reached a maximum of 1267 in the 1830's. Castle Drogo, although ancient in appearance, was not finally completed until 1930 nineteen years after the foundation stone was laid. Although still occupied by the Drewe family it was given to The National Trust in 1973 and is now open to the public.

The charming Drewe Arms is unique, it is probably the most original pub in Devon if not in England. The licensee, "Aunt Mable" as she is affectionally known, is the longest serving landlady in the country and has been at the Drewe Arms since 1919. When I visited the pub in 1992, and had the pleasure of speaking to her, she was in her 97th year and still very much the boss. She lives in her own room at one end of the pub whilst the other end is open to the public. The one simple room has part boarded walls, a small fireplace, tables, chairs, wooden wall seats and a dart board. A door leads through to a smaller room where the drinks are kept.

There is cider and one real ale, Flowers I.P.A, drawn straight from the barrel.

Food is limited to a choice of either delicious home cooked ham sandwiches made from very fresh, hand cut wholemeal bread or tasty bread and cheese with pickle. In todays busy world I wonder how much longer pubs like this can survive in their present form, I would like to think for many more years to come but I fear economics will ultimately dictate their future. Let us all appreciate them while we can.

Weekday opening times are from 10.30 a.m. till 2.30 p.m. and 6.p.m. till 11 p.m. Telephone: (0647) 21224.

Village is signed from the A382 north from Moretonhampstead.

Approx. distance of walk: 5 miles. O.S.Map 191 SX 736/908.

Park where you can in the village centre.

My favourite walk in Devon which although delightful at any time of the year is probably at its best in late spring when the wild flowers are in full bloom. The scenery along The Hunters Path below Castle Drogo is quite breathtaking and the river path to Fingle Bridge is one of the most picturesque I know. Although steep in places the going is easy, all the paths are well marked and in very good condition a credit to the National Trust who maintain them. Of interest to campers or caraveners wishing to stay in the area there is a is a lovely site at Clifford Bridge. Sited beside the River Teign in a peaceful, picturesque wooded valley it must surely be one of the most attractives sites in Devon.

From the village take the Moretonhampstead road and in just a short distance turn left on to the public bridle path signed, To Fingle Bridge. Walk to the bottom and into The Castle Drogo Estate. Take the path on the right signed, To Hunters Path. Stepped in part, it climbs steeply up to a gate allowing access to the field ahead. Keeping close to the boundary proceed towards a couple of stiles and down to the finger post turning right onto the Hunters Path.

The views from this path are quite outstanding. Mixed woods cover the hillsides which rise steeply up from the Teign Valley. In places granite outcrops jut prominently from the hillside. If you wish to visit Castle Drogo take the signed diversion. The Castle is open daily, except Friday, from 11 a.m. till 5.30 p.m. The path skirts the base of the castle before joining with a farm track.

Turn left then left again after the cattle grid. Keep walking until you reach the river but do not cross the bridge instead turn left on to the Fisherman's Path. It is a beautiful path running beside the river for about a mile and a half until it reaches Fingle Bridge. In spring and summer there are many wild flowers to be seen including large displays of Bluebells. The Anglers Rest is a good half-way refreshment stop.

From the bridge turn left and further ahead take the footpath on the left signed, To The Hunters Path. Narrow and uneven in places, the path rises quite steeply up to join with The Hunters Path. Turn right at the finger post signed, To Drewsteignton. After a while the path descends into Drewsteignton Wood - welcome shade on a hot sunny day. Turn right at the track and follow it until you again reach the finger post at the start of the walk retracing your steps back up the track to the village.

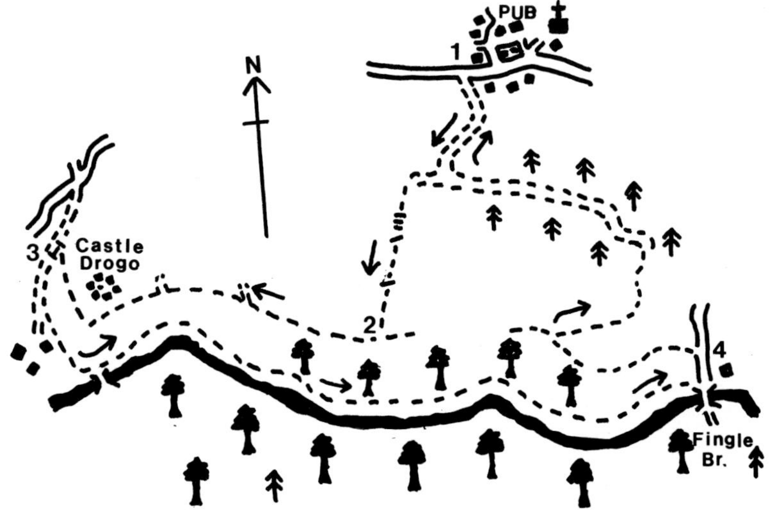

The Angler's Rest

The Fisherman's Path

The Royal Oak, Dunsford

The Royal Oak is a Victorian pub rebuilt following a devastating fire. It last changed hands as recently as 1991 and is now personally run by the friendly new owners, Guy and Alison who have plans to gradually restore the interior.

Rooms lead off from the central bar, one is a cosy dining area the other a comfortable lounge heated by a warm wood burning stove set in a large stone fireplace. There is a pool room down a short flight of steps, a rear courtyard and a sunny beer garden. Evening entertainment is often arranged in the bar and on some Tuesdays a hairdresser is on hand to offer his services.

The inn is a freehouse and prides itself on the quality and variety of the real ales served. With the option of drinking from a two pint tankard, you can choose between Marston's Pedigree and Boddingtons Bitter plus guest ales which might include Tally Ho Bitter, Shepherd Neame Best Bitter, Ash Vine Tanker and Brains Bitter.

Bar snacks can range from homemade soup and ploughman's to a chip buttie. Alongside the main menu, which offers traditional fare such as steak and kidney pie and beef wellington there are tempting daily specials like Italian beef and pasta bake, fish casserole and sticky pork spare ribs served on a bed of rice. Vegetarians can enjoy mushroom stroganoff, bubble and squeak, broccoli and Stilton quiche, vegetable chilli and cheese and tomato pie. And for the sweet toothed banana cooked in brandy with lemon, orange juice and clotted cream.

The inn is open in the week from 11.30 a.m. till 2.30/3 p.m. and from 6/6.30 p.m. till 11 p.m. Both children and dogs are welcome. Comfortable accommodation is available in a converted barn.

Telephone: (0647) 52256.

Dunsford is just inside the north eastern perimeter of The Dartmoor National Park signed from the B3212 between Exeter and Moretonhampstead. The pub is next to the church.

Approx. distance of walk: 5 miles. O.S.Map No.191 SX 812/892.

Although the inn does have a small car park opposite, one can park safely in the lane at the front.

A most enjoyable, scenic walk which takes you south from Dunsford across the Teign on the stepping stone bridge, through the lovely Bridford Woods, owned by The National Trust and to Steps Bridge, built in 1816. The woodlands are of a mixed deciduous type which, until the beginning of the century, were cut every 25 years for fencing and to make charcoal. The area is famous for its wild flowers and to see them at their best try to walk in April or May. After leaving the woods the walk continues along peaceful country, crosses the Teign for a second time and follows a delightful bridleway up to Sowton Barton after which a footpath descends across fields and through woods back to the village. Although there are some demanding steep sections the going is generally easy and mostly dry underfoot. For a shorter walk of just under 3 miles, which avoids the stepping stone bridge, you can start from the Steps Bridge Inn south of Dunsford on the B3212. The National Trust have a free car park next to the pub. Start from paragraph 3 in the text.

Turn right from the pub, and after about one hundred yards, turn left into the cul-de-sac. Walk to the bottom and take the narrow footpath beside the house, over the stile into the field and straight across to the corner. Turn right into the field and walk down beside the hedge to the stile crossing into the adjoining field. Make your way down to gate at the bottom and turn right into the lane. Just beyond Dunsford Mill Country House Hotel take the footpath on the left signed, To Britford Wood.

Walk down beside the house to the river, go across on the stepping stones and keep straight ahead into the wood turning right on the signed path to Steps Bridge. Bear left at the house following the narrow path up beside the fence and keep to the main path ahead, ignoring the side tracks. Cut into the hillside it is an attractive path running high above the Teign eventually bringing you out to the Steps Bridge Inn - a lovely refreshment stop.

The Steps Bridge Inn

The stepping stones across the Teign

The bridleway from Sowton Mill

Enter the woods and turn right onto the bridleway signed, To Burnicombe for Bridford. Cross the wooden footbridge and follow either path into the woods. In May the smell of garlic from the Ransoms can be almost overpowering. Again cross the stream and take the bridleway on the left and further ahead fork right. Turn left at the top along the path close to the field boundary then turn right at the cross track, through the gate into the lane and turn left.

It is a very attractive, peaceful lane carrying little or no traffic. After about a mile, as you approach a sharp right-hand bend, there is a drive way on the left leading to Mill House, the footpath is signed, "To Steps Bridge via Britford Wood". Take this path if you are on the short walk or indeed if you wish to retrace your steps back to Dunsford.

Carry on along the lane and upon reaching the next right-hand bend you will see a small wooden gate beside the driveway to Swannaford House. To cut the cornergo into the field and bear right down across to the drive, out into the lane and turn left. Cross the road bridge and take the footpath on the right signed, to Sowton Mill. Pass between the dwellings then look for the narrow path on the left rising steeply up into the woods. It is a beautiful path abundant with numerous wild flowers. After passing through the gates into the field, walk round, up to the lane and turn left.

In fifty yards turn left through the gate onto the signed footpath. It is very scenic with stunning views. Pass through the gate on the left and continue down, through another gate, bearing left in the direction of the waymark across to the stile in the far corner. Walk beside the hedge then cross the stile into the wood following the path down to the road and turn left. Keep walking until you reach the stile on the right opposite the lay-by.

Follow the path up then over the stile into the adjoining field walking across close to the wire fence, over a couple more stiles and into the field. Keeping close to the hedge, make you way to the track at the top, walk up to the lane and turn left back to the pub.

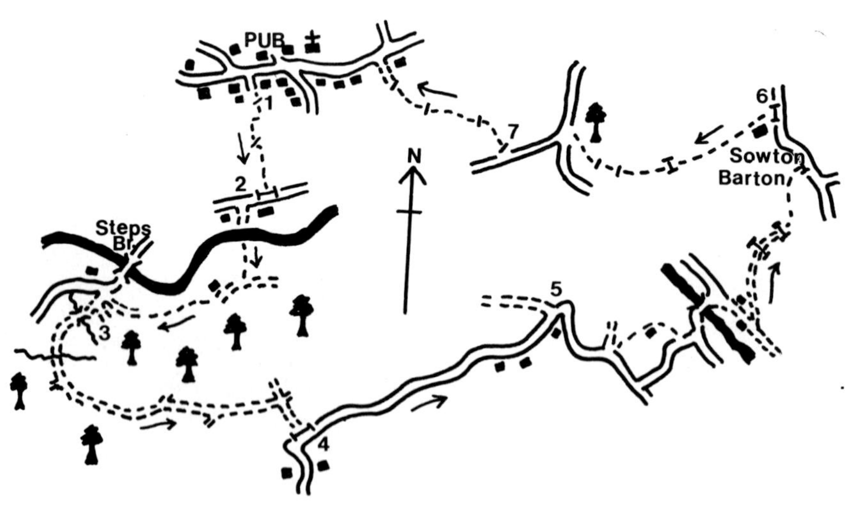

The sketch maps in this book are not necessarily to scale but have been drawn to show the maximum amount of detail.

Pyne Arms, East Down

For a small hamlet East Down is well served by a very good pub. Situated in a delightful spot it is well away from passing traffic and surrounded by green hills. A telephone kiosk occupies part of the beer garden evidence, that until quite recently, it was the village post office. The building itself is some three hundred years old a fact which becomes more evident once inside. The cosy main bar is comfortably furnished and has a low beamed ceiling. An archway leads through to a separate seating area to the side of which is a pool room with a flagstone floor.

The inn is a freehouse, one of a group of four "Exmoor Inns". Two Whitbread real ales presently available are Castle Eden Ale and Flowers I.P.A.

The inn is open for food seven days a week. There is a large menu to choose from with additional daily specials and vegetarian dishes listed on the blackboards. Apart from the usual snacks such as homemade soup, sandwiches, ploughman's and tasty burgers the pub has its own recipe German sausage made from 100% veal and pork. Other meals include home cooked ham and eggs, sauted chicken breast in mushroom, cream and white wine sauce, beef stroganoff, prime English veal escallops, several pasta dishes and sauteed fillet of beef in red wine, green peppercorn and mushroom sauce. Every Thursday, Friday and Saturday evening all steaks are cooked on the "CHARGRILL". Fish dishes are popular such as seafood thermidor but in particular mussels when in season which are served in four different ways. One recipe is mussels Provencal they are cooked with onions, mushrooms, garlic, tomatoes, wine and spices. Tasty sauces are served with many of the meals and if you like a particular one you can buy some to take away.

Children under the age of 14 are not permitted in the bar but dogs are allowed with the permission of the management. Weekday opening times are from 11 a.m. till 2.30 p.m. and 6 p.m. till 11 p.m.

Telephone: (0271) 850207.

East Down is signed from the A39 between Barnstaple and Lynton.

Approx. distance of walk: 3.5 miles. O.S.Map 180 SS 600/415.

The Inn has its own large car park opposite.

A very scenic walk which can be demanding in places. After following a peaceful country lane a track leads into woods. The path then crosses the River Yeo and continues across farm land and along lanes and tracks.

Turn right from the pub up, past the church of St John the baptist and keep straight ahead at the bend towards Bugford. When you reach the track on the right, opposite the house, walk down to the gate, pass between the farm buildings and bear right through the gate into the field. Keeping close to the slate wall on the left, proceed down to the gate and follow the track through the woods to the gate on the other side. Go through and bear right down the field to the bridge at the bottom. After crossing the stream head up the field and turn left on to the rough track beside the woods. Walk up to the gate, pass between the buildings, out onto the drive and turn right.

After a few paces turn left through the gate into the field walking straight ahead, through the gap into the field ahead and across to one more gate before bearing left down the field to the wooden crossing point. Go out into the lane, turn left and cross the bridge. As you round the bend enter the drive on the right to Milwood Barn then immediately go through the metal gate on the right and follow the path ahead. Pass through the wooden gate into the field and, keeping close to the hedge, follow the path through the small gate and continue walking until you reach the stile in the hedge allowing access to the adjoining field then turn left. A raised path runs through the valley and exits through a gate on to a rough stone track. Turn left walking round and up into the field. The footpath follows the field boundary up to a gate on the right and then crosses more farm land in an arc eventually reaching the drive to the farm.

Turn left when you reach the lane, then keep straight ahead at the next bend on to the track signed, to Shortacombe. After entering the driveway turn left onto the narrow grass track by the side of the house leading up to a gate set in a high wire fence. Go through into the field and bear left aiming for the far corner. Climb the ladder stile down to the narrow path beside the hedge, turn right and then cross into the field on the left carefully descending down the stone steps. Walk straight across to the gap then bear right down to the farm gate and out to the track back down to the pub.

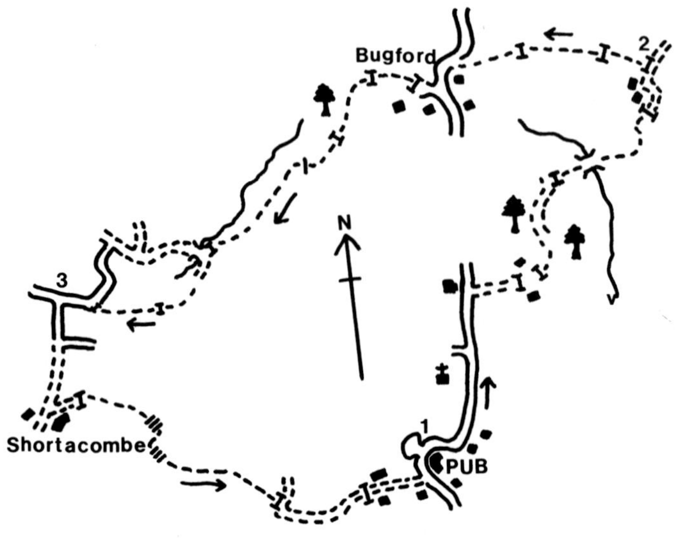

Looking west towards Bolt Head, Walk No. 15

Rockham Bay, Mortehoe, Walk No. 26

The Providence Inn, East Prawle

East Prawle is the southernmost village in Devon and although quite small is well served with two pubs, The Pigs Nose, opposite the village green, and the Providence Inn in the lane behind. Built in the 18th century it is a genuine village local. Four small rooms were knocked through to form the present open plan bar explanation for the pub having four fireplaces, the largest has a warm log fire in winter. Furnishings simply consist of window seats, stick back chairs, elm tables and a large wooden settle close to the fire. There is a separate dining room and a pretty beer garden at the back with views of the sea.

The inn is a freehouse personally run by the friendly owners, Bryan and Eve Gill. The two real ales presently served are Dartmoor Best and Wadworth 6X.

Good home cooked food is served all week but mostly snacks at lunchtime such as homemade soup, ploughman's, pasties, jacket potatoes and sandwiches. Daily blackboard specials, which might include homemade chicken korma or home-made chicken pie are supplemented by garlic mushrooms seafood au gratin, vegetable biriani, cod and chips and a ham salad. The inn offers a selection of special meals for which advanced booking is advisable. A crab supper being one example, the other a three course Sunday roast. Tempting homemade sweets range from treacle tart to cider and apple cake.

Children are allowed in the restaurant and dogs in the bar on a lead. Weekday opening times are flexible dependant upon trade but during the summer season the pub usually is open all day from 11 a.m. till 11 p.m. Bed and Breakfast is available.

Telephone: (054851) 208.

Remotely situated East Prawle is signed from the A379 east from Kingsbridge. The inn is in the lane north from the village green.

Approx. distance of walk: 3.5 miles. O.S.Map 202 SX 781/365.

Park outside the pub or by the village green.

A very enjoyable and scenic coastal walk down to Gammon Head and Prawle Point - the most southerly part of Devon. After following the coastal path an attractive bridlepath takes you steeply back up to the village. Whilst mostly dry underfoot parts of the walk are quite rugged and steep in places especially the steps on the coast path.

Leave the pub turning left and then right into the lane walking for about half a mile until you reach the bend then keep straight ahead onto the gravel track signed, Gammon Head 1 mile. At the end of the track pass through the gate into the field and cross to the gate on the far side. Walk up the narrow grass path and turn right onto the track.

Cross the stile following the path towards Gammon Head. Fork right at the path sign down to the lower path and continue round close to the cliff edge. In places the path is very uneven and a little care is necessary to pick your way around the rocks. Masses of wild flowers grow on the cliff face including the wild Geranium.

Negotiate the stone wall, cross the stile and turn left. Cross a second stile into the field and walk to the stile at the bottom to rejoin the path beside the shore. After following the headland, passing through more gates and crossing a few more stiles, you will eventually reach a finger post directing you inland up a track signed, To East Prawle. At the finger post turn right and follow the narrow path up to the lane then steeply back up the hill to the pub.

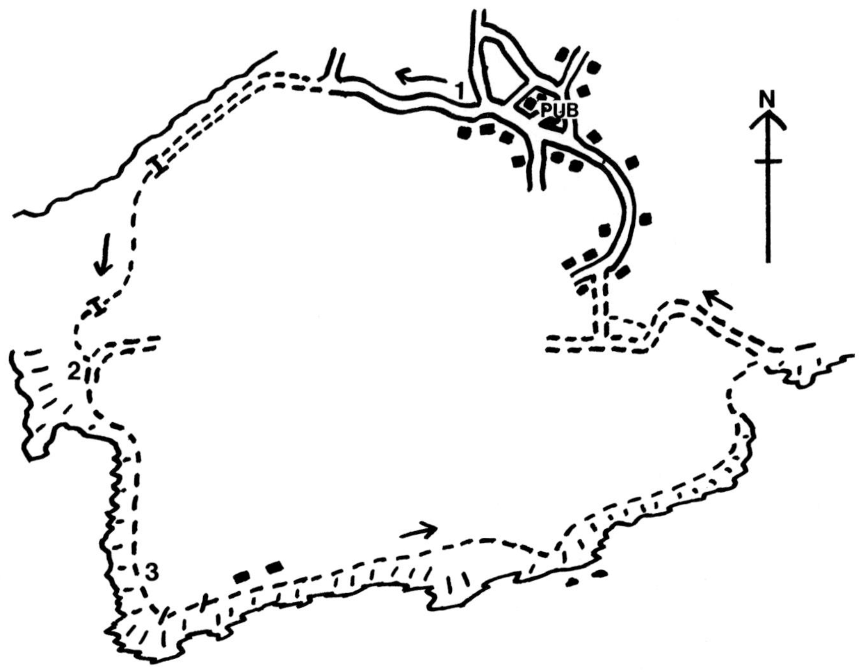

Hartland Quay Hotel, Hartland Quay

Hartland Quay has had a very long history built after an act of Parliament in December 1566. The old pier has long since been claimed by the sea but photographs of how it once looked can be seen in the museum or in a small publication entitled, Hartland Quay - The Story of a Vanished Port. Visitors come here from all parts of the globe drawn by the rugged scenery and the unspoilt character of this part of Devon.

The Hartland Quay Hotel originally housed the merchant or tenant of the quay and the present "Green Ranger Bar" were the stables. Aptly designed in a nautical theme photographs of wrecks, portholes and other artifacts claimed from the many ships that have come to grief on the jagged rocks below, decorate the interior; most notably a line of brass portholes from the S.S. Green Ranger wrecked as recently as 1962. Outside at the front is a row of picnic benches in a sunny but sheltered spot. I imagine it was because of its peaceful location that Hartland Quay was chosen by Walt Disney when making Treasure Island. The pirates from the Galleon Appledore were landed on the beach below whilst at the same time a staring role was given to the hotel as the Benbow Inn.

The hotel is a freehouse and part of the Stucley Estate. Well conditioned Tinners Ale, from the St Austell Brewery, is delivered by hand pump. Although small the menu offers a varied choice of generous bar meals such as a "fisherman's snack" consisting of soup bread and cheese also sandwiches, ploughman's, pasties, steak and kidney pie, lasagne, fish and chips, jacket potatoes and salads.

Weekday opening times are from 11 a.m till 2.45 p.m and 6.30 p.m. till 11 p.m. Families are welcome and dogs too if kept under control. Accommodation is available in the hotel.

Telephone: (0237) 441218.

From the A39 between Barnstaple and Kilkhampton take the B3248, signed to Hartland, and continue through the village to eventually reach the Quay.

Approx. distance of walk: 3.5 miles. O.S. Map 190 SS 223/247.

There is a large car park at the bottom of the cliffs by the pub but a small charge is made for entry.

This very scenic walk at first takes you south along the rugged coast path to the impressive waterfalls at Speke's Mill Mouth. After which the path heads inland rising steeply up to Kernstone Cross and along a lane into the hamlet of Stoke. From here the path crosses farm land back to the quay.

From the car park beside the pub make your way up the signed footpath round the cliff edge to the fingerpost. Turn right down the steps to the kissing gate and follow the path ahead and behind St Catherine's Tor. Step stone the stream and bear left across the field to the gateway. Follow the path up the bank, over the wall and head down to Speke's Mill Mouth. The series of waterfalls, the highest being 53 feet, are a magnificent sight tumbling down to the shore.

Head inland along the track past the sand lews. (bays once used to grade sand brought from the beach by donkeys). Fork left and continue up the track, past the house turning right into the lane then left at the crossroads. Beyond the farm the lane soon deteriorates into a rough stone track. After crossing the bridge over Wargery Water continue ahead along the lane to Stoke and bear left into the churchyard.

The church, whose patron is St Nectan, dates from the fourteenth century. At 128 feet the tower, which served as a landmark for sailors, is the second tallest parish church tower in Devon. Walk to the back of the church, climb the stone wall and turn right on to the signed footpath. It runs beside the road past houses before entering a field. Keep close to the hedge on the left unless you wish to make a detour up to the ruined rocket house. Leave the field by the house and turn right to pick up the path down the hillside joining the lane back to the pub.

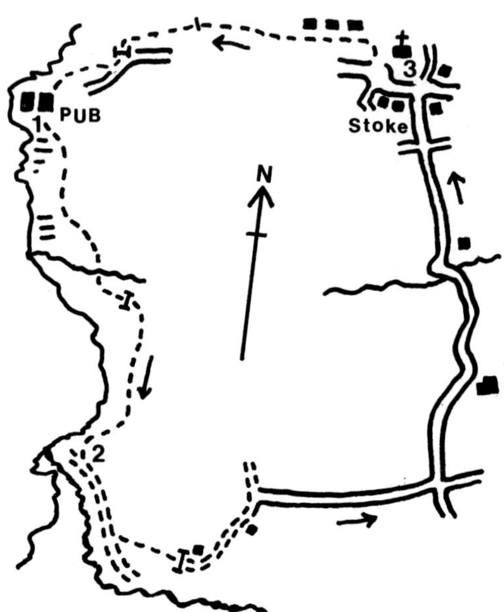

The Hunters' Inn, Heddon's Mouth

In 1868 a family of farmers named Berry became tenants of the thatched cottage that once occupied the present site of the inn. They served beer from their kitchen which had by now become an inn in the true sense. In 1895 the village postman on his round noticed smoke coming from the thatch but by the time he raised the alarm it was too late, within minutes the building was a ruin. The following year the foundations were laid for the present pub and it was completed several years later in the style of a Swiss chalet.

Situated in The Heddon Valley, an area of outstanding natural beauty, this homely inn is comfortably furnished with a warm log fire in winter. Hung on the walls are many old photographs including some of the thatched inn before the fire. Peacocks roam free outside and if you are lucky display there magnificent tail feathers. A children's room is to be found to the rear of the bar, and there are tables and chairs in the garden at the front.

The inn is a freehouse well run by the amiable owner, Chris Moate. The well stocked bar has three real ales Wadworth 6X, Burton Ale and Tetley Bitter. Local scrumpy is available during the summer.

The Buttery serves a wide range of hot and cold food at lunchtime between 12 noon and 2 p.m. Afternoon tea is served between 3 p.m. and 5 p.m. and "The Pheasantry" restaurant opens from 7 p.m. The constantly changing food menu might include starters of seafood on a shell au gratin or mushrooms in garlic with a cheese dip followed by salmon with asparagus, half a roast duck - crispy and part boned, various steaks and homemade lasagne. Also each day there are several specials listed on the blackboard.

Well behaved children are welcome and dogs too if kept on a lead. Weekday opening times can be flexible. From April to November the inn is open all day from 11 a.m. till 11 p.m, closing between 3 p.m. and 7 p.m. for the rest of the year. Accommodation is available throughout the year.

Telephone: (059 83) 230.

Hunters' Inn is signed from the A39 between Combe Martin and Lynton.

Approx. distance of walk: 5 miles. O.S. Map 180 SS 655/482.

Park anywhere in the lane.

A favourite of mine this delightful, scenic walk is in one of the most beautiful and unspoilt areas of Exmoor. Although a bit demanding in places the going is generally good, dry underfoot and on well maintained footpaths making it ideal for all the family.

Go up the stony track beside the inn signed, Martinhoe, Woody Bay and Heddon's Mouth, pass through the gate and take the left fork, signed To Heddon's Mouth. After 250 yards fork left down to the river. Lush vegetation and many wild flowers carpet the banks and hillside. Ignore the bridge across the river but continue walking until you reach the path on the right signed, to Woody Bay Beach.

After crossing Hill Brook a steep climb takes you to Highveer Point where you have a lovely view down to Heddon's Mouth and the old lime kiln. The path continues to climb steadily through large areas of coastal heath which are a riot of colour in August. It is very peaceful, very scenic and totally unspoilt. After rounding The Beacon the path descends past the waterfall at Hollow Brook and up to a stile allowing access to an oak wood, owned by The National Trust. Leave by the stile and, unless you want to visit Woody Bay, bear right up the drive to the lane. Turn right, and after rounding the bend, go up the path to the left of the gate (not through the gate). At the top turn right to Martinhoe with its 11th century church.

A quarter of a mile beyond the hamlet you reach a short grass track on the right leading down to a farm gate. Go through into the field, and keeping fairly close to the hedge boundary, walk across to the far hedge and turn left. Follow the attractive path to the bottom, go through the small wooden gate and follow the path beside the stream on the left. Pass through the gate then walk up the drive to the lane turning right down to the pub.

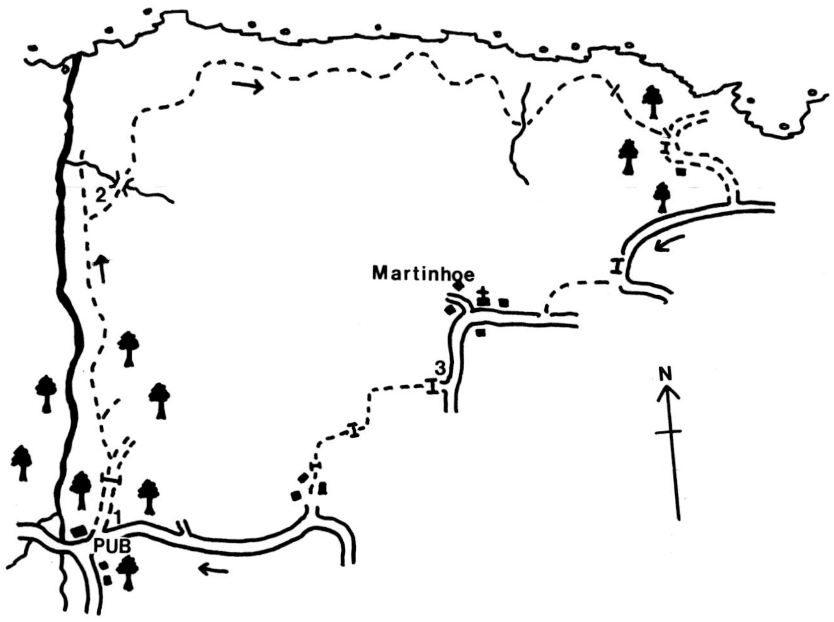

Elephant's Nest, Horndon

Originally miners cottages, dating from the 16th century the Elephant's Nest first became an inn at the beginning of this century and was known at that time as The New Inn having replaced the original village pub. A past landlord, who was a fairly portly gentleman with a very large beard, always sat behind the bar. One day a customer suggested he looked like an elephant sitting on his nest, from then on it was decided to adopt the present name.

Bare stone walls, darkened by countless fires and a polished slate floor are features of the main bar whilst ancient beams support the close boarded ceiling. Furnishings are a mix of padded wall seats, church pews, stools and country chairs. There is an equally attractive dining room, a small family room and a beer garden with picnic benches.

The inn is a freehouse very well run by the friendly owners, Nick and Gill Hamer and Peta Hughes. Regular real ales include Boddingtons Bitter, Webster's Yorkshire and Palmers Traditional Bitter plus a gust such as Botwrights Man o War brewed in Ashburton.

A good choice of bar food, which includes a number of vegetarian dishes, is chalked daily on the blackboard. The lunchtime menu offers soup, ploughman's, filled cob rolls, cheese and tomato quiche and butter bean bake. On my last visit there was also black eyed beans and mushrooms, grilled hake, cheese and spinach quiche, ratatouille with cheese and Bucks bacon bodger and on the evening menu prawn Waldorf, giant cheesy mussels and peanut and lentil roulade, plus the old favourites steak and kidney and game pie. The large selection of sweets are all served with local clotted cream.

Weekday opening times are from 11.30 a.m. till 2.30 p.m. and 6.30 p.m. till 11 p.m. Children are allowed in either of the two rooms away from the bar and there is no objection to dogs. Overnight accommodation is available.

Telephone: (0822) 810273.

Situated on the western edge of Dartmoor, Horndon is signed from the A386 at Mary Tavy.

Approx. distance of walk: 2.75 miles. O.S.Map 191 SX 517/800.

The inn has its own car park but there is some limited parking in the lane at the front.

A short but very enjoyable, easy going walk at first on an attractive footpath beside a leat into woods and then along a lovely bridlepath to Zoar before returning on a moor land road.

From the inn turn right then right again into the lane by the telephone kiosk. Keep bearing right as the lane merges into a track and then narrows to a stony path. Before reaching the bottom cross the stile into the field on the left and follow the raised path beside the leat. Many leats were constructed in the area to supply water to work the machinery in the engine houses at the mines. There are a few stiles and gates to negotiate before the path enters a wood. The steep banks on either side are very lush and green with ferns and wild flowers growing in abundance through the moss covered ground.

After about a mile of easy walking you reach the sluice gate where a metal ladder takes you up to the lane. Turn left, and left again at the bend passing through the farm gate onto the bridleway. It is signed "To the Road Near Creason". Keep to the main track before one last gate brings you out to an area of open moor. Walk across towards the dwellings and up round to the lane turning left back to the pub.

The sketch maps in this book are not necessarily to scale but have been drawn to show the maximum amount of detail.

The Royal Inn, Horsebridge

Horsebridge is just a small sleepy hamlet beside the River Tamar but has not always been that way. The bridge, from which the area takes its name, was constructed in 1437 by the monks and was the first to be built over the Tamar. Many people would of used the route and probably stopped at the inn for refreshment. Built first as a nunnery it was later turned into an inn known as The Packhorse, the name was subsequently changed following a visit by Charles I.

There are two bars in this delightful, unspoilt local both heated by log fires in the winter. The simply furnished "Village Bar" has stone walls, a slate floor and sensibly placed bar games at one end, whilst the cosier lounge has a partioned dining area, a separate side room behind the stone fireplace and lots of interesting regalia decorating the walls. On fine days you can sit on the front terrace overlooking the river or in the attractive side garden.

The pub is unique as it brews its own beer a tradition started by a previous landlord in 1962 and continued by the present owners, Terry and Julie Wood. On sale are three of their own real ales Heller, Horsebridge Best and the stronger Tamar Bitter plus three guests Marstons Pedigree, Draught Bass and Royal Oak.

Very good bar food is available everyday except Sunday evening. Chalked on blackboards above the bar the lunchtime menu lists a dozen different ploughman's and pot meals of lasagagne, herby sausage bake and cottage pie. Vegetarians might be tempted by mushroom and nut fettuccine, Raj vegetable curry, leek and Stilton bake or country vegetable pie. For those wanting something a bit different there is lamb provencal, near eastern pork, half a smoked chicken, and stir fried kidneys plus a daily special like salmon with garlic and fine herbs.

Weekday opening times are from 12 noon till 2.30 p.m. and 7 p.m. till 11 p.m. Children under 14 are not allowed inside the pub and dogs are only permitted in the Village Bar on a lead.

Telephone: (082 287) 214.

This remote and tiny hamlet is bounded by the A388, the A390 and the A384, just inside the Devon border. Although it can be reached from all three main roads the lanes are narrow and not very well signed. The most direct route is south from the A384 at Milton Green.

Approx. distance of walk: 3.5 miles. O.S.Map 201 SX 401/749.

There is ample parking at the side of the inn, at the front and in the lane.

The first half of the walk takes you up an attractive gully to Townlake then along country lanes, across farm land and through woods. After passing through the small hamlet of Sydenham Damerel you can return down the lane or retrace your steps through Townlake.

Turn left from the inn and left again walking away from the bridge. In twenty yards take the signed public footpath on the left. It is an attractive gully shaded by an overhead tree canopy where many wild flowers and ferns flourish, especially Primroses. Pass through the two kissing gates and head up the field, out through the kissing gate at the top turning right into the lane.

In 200 hundred yards leave the lane and take the track on the left, up to the gate at the end and keep straight ahead across the field to the crossing point in the wall. Go over into the field on the left, and bearing left, walk across to the exit point in the far hedge leading down to the lane. The exact line across the field to the hedge is not obvious but hopefully will be signed by the time of publication. Turn left, past the dwellings and proceed down the hill until you reach the signed footpath on the left.

Go through the gate and follow the track, through a second gate, and in twenty paces, turn left through the small gate following

the signed path up the bank to the stile. Turn right on to the track keeping to the raised path above the meadow. Although it can become overgrown in summer eventually you will find it leads up to a farm gate. Continue ahead then cross the stile onto the woodland path. Again there is an abundance of springtime wild flowers especially primroses. Leave the woods by the stile and continue up the path and into the field walking round beside the hedge and out through the farm gate.

Cross the lane towards Lane End then turn left at the track. At the bend go over the stile into the field ahead and continue in the same direction, through three more gates and out into the lane. Turn left through the village then right when you reach the lane. Horsebridge is signed $\frac{1}{2}$ mile but part way down the lane there is a signed path on the left which cuts across the fields to Townlake enabling you to retrace your steps down the field to the gully.

Duke of York, Iddesleigh

Happily in Devon there are still a few old village pubs where visitors and locals can rub shoulders in a relaxed and comfortable atmosphere and where one can sit in front of an open fire and still enjoy a good pint of real ale drawn traditionally straight from the barrel.

The lovely thatched, Duke of York, which dates from the 14th century, is one of my favourites. Largely unspoilt the main bar, mellow with age, has a beamed ceiling and bare stone walls. Simple furnishings consist of scrubbed tables, assorted chairs and window seats. Hung on the wall, in a small seating area partioned from the main bar, is an interesting photograph taken in 1911 showing villagers on the Iddesleigh Club walk. There is a separate cosy dining room, also with a large open fire and a small beer garden reached through the old coach arch at the side.

The inn is a freehouse personally run by the owners, Diane and Andrew King who only took over in July 1992. There are two well conditioned real ales, Old Hooky - an unusual tawny beer from The Hook Norton Brewery and Cotleigh Tawny Bitter.

A good choice of bar meals are available all cooked on the premises by Martin Gent, nephew of the owners. In addition to sandwiches and ploughman's the list, chalked daily on the blackboard, might include homemade soup, steak and kidney pie, whole grilled plaice, lasagne, various steaks, scampi, ham egg and chips, tasty homemade sausages and pan fried chicken with herbs and butter plus a vegetarian dish. Sweets range from sticky toffee pudding to chocolate torte.

Monday to Saturday the inn is open all day from 11.30 a.m. till 11.00 p.m. Children are welcome in the two rooms at either end of the bar and there is no objection to dogs on a lead. Overnight accommodation is available in the pub or the adjacent cottage.

Telephone: (0837) 810253.

Iddesleigh is a remote village on the B3217 which runs south from the A377 to Okehampton.

Approx. distance of walk: 3 miles. O.S. Map 191 SS 570/083.

Park in the road at the front.An enjoyable walk across farm land and along peaceful country lanes. The path from Iddesleigh to Upcott now forms part of the The Tarka Trail.

From the inn walk down to the road, turn left and keep straight ahead on to the gravel track. Enter the farm and immediately turn left following the track round, through the gate and up to the lane. Cross the road at Coombe Cottage onto the track opposite and keep walking until the entrance to Coombe Farm is reached. Look for a wooden gate on the left with a left and right way-mark affixed then follow the left-hand path walking down across the field towards some trees and bushes which conceal a stile and footbridge across a small stream. Cross into the field and climb up to the metal gate which is some two thirds up the left-hand boundary fence. Go through the gate and walk up diagonally to the top corner of the field where two metal gates allow access to the farm track. Continue up to the lane and turn left into Upcott.

The walk down hill affords some magnificent views across the valley. At the bottom the road meets the B3217 at a T junction. Turn left here and proceed uphill for a short way turning left at a large Babtist church, the road is signed to Whitemore and Hennacroft. Walk to the brow of the hill and look for a public footpath sign on the right. Bear right across this field to a large metal gate. On the way there are good views of St James Church. Pass through the gate and head down to one last gate in the far hedge, out onto the track and turn right back to the pub.

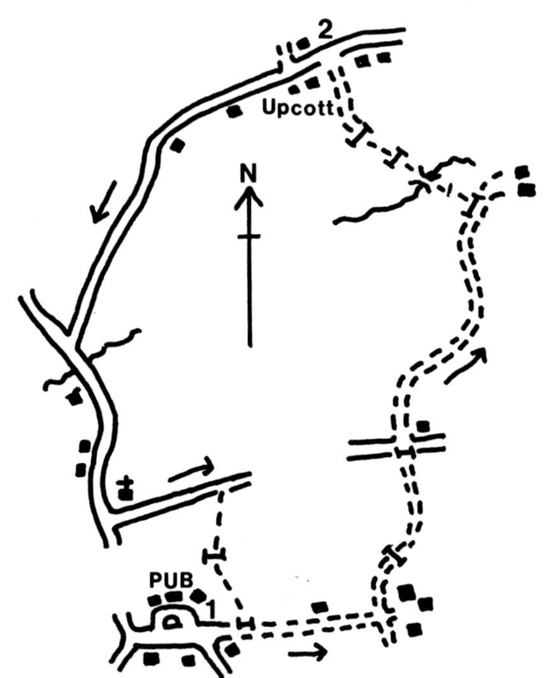

The Marisco Tavern, Lundy

Owned by The National Trust, Lundy Island is leased to the Landmark Trust a charity established in 1965 and set up to save and restore the few buildings. Puffins breed annually on the Island which has a long history the name itself being Norse for puffin. More recently the island was bought in 1836 by William Hudson Heaven who built Millcombe House. Today only a handful of people live and work on the island which they share with sheep, cattle, horses, a colony of grey seals and a herd of wild Soay sheep, blissfully there are no cars.

Lundy is unique, the island is large enough to have a genuine life of its own, small enough to offer the peace and tranquility for those wishing to escape the fast pace of life today. It is a magical place and all who go say they experience a mild elevation.

The Marisco Tavern, named after one of the old owner families, is an excellent pub well run by the licensees, Linzi and Nigel the attractive main bar is simply furnished and heated by an open wood fire. There are more tables in the upstairs gallery and in the adjoining store. Lots of ships artifacts adorn the stone walls a reminder of the many wrecks claimed by the island over the centuries. High up on the wall a wind indicator records the electricity generated by the islands windmill - the only power supply other then diesel generators. A separate fish restaurant supplies the best of the daily catch.

Two real ales presently available are Burton Ale and Benskins Best Bitter but the inn has its own small brewery and will shortly start brewing again.

Lunch time bar snacks include sandwiches, ploughman's, filled babs etc. In the evening a more comprehensive menu is available offering some 26 dishes. Round the world platters are a feature and there are also ten vegetarian meals plus three daily specials.

Opening times are from 12 noon till 2 p.m. and 6 p.m. till 11/11.30 p.m, unless a boat arrives when the pub is open all day. Children and dogs are both welcome.

Telephone: (0237) 431831.

Lundy can only be reached by boat. The M.S.Oldenburg, the island's passenger and supply ship, runs throughout the year from Bideford and also from Ilfracombe in the summer season. The journey takes about two hours. There are sailings on most Saturdays and Wednesdays throughout the year with limited sailings on the other days except Sunday. A timetable and price list can be obtained in advance from The Landmark Trust at Shottesbrooke, Maidenhead, Berks SL6 3SW. Tel.(0628 82) 5925.

Approx. distance of walk: 6 miles or as short a distance as you want to make it. O.S.Map 180 SS 136/441.

There is ample car parking at both ports.

Lundy measures only one mile at its widest point and is just over three miles in length so a complete round trip of the island is only a little over 6 miles. The scenery is stunningly beautiful. The steep rugged clifs on the west side are a dramatic contrast to the gentler slopes of the eastern side with their lush vegetation whilst the top is almost flat. Everybody has the free run of the island so having bought a map you can plan your own route. The walk I followed took in some of the best scenery and several points of interest.

There is no jetty on Lundy so the first task is to get everyone on to the beach. This is done by small motor launch which shuttles passengers to and from a mobile landing stage. Once on the beach make your way across to the track and up the cliff. At Millcombe House go on to the path at the back walking up to the inn at the top. It is fairly steep in places and strong footwear is recommended. Leave the Tavern and head north through the farm following the track. After passing Quarter Wall a track bears right down to Belle Vue cottages. I took the path north along the cliff face. It is very scenic, very peaceful with lots of colourful vegetation including Lundy cabbage a plant unique to the island, interesting rock pools and dramatic rock formations to be seen. I walked as far Gannets Coombe and watched the seals playing in the bay below.

From here I climbed the cliff and crossed the island to the North Light. To visit the point necessitates walking down a long flight of steps, worth though it for the scenery. It is at this end of the island that you are more likely to see the wild Soay sheep. Return along the main track down the centre of the island. It is easy going passing close to the marshes, the lake and the remains of an aircraft that crash landed during the last war. Before reaching the farm take the track westwards past the wind generator towards the old light and after passing through the ancient cemetery continue south. A scenic path follows the cliff round the point and down to the ruined castle from whence you can return, past the church back to the tavern.

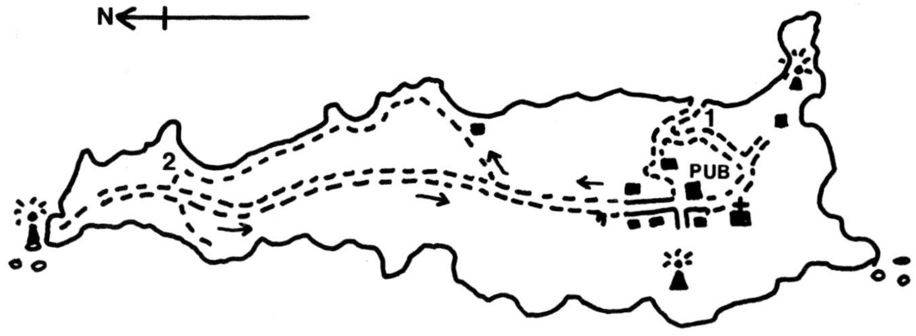

Luppitt Inn, Luppitt

Driving into Luppitt one enters the peace and quiet of yesteryear. This small, unspoilt East Devon village is still very much a local community with many of its residents related in some way or other. In the heart of the village is The Luppitt Inn one of the simplest pubs in the County.

Previously known as The Red Lion it is essentially still a farmhouse selling ale. Owned by her parents, and grandparents before them, Mary took over the licence in 1989 from her husband, Archie Wright who was the licensee for many years. There are just two rooms, the small simply furnished bar and an additional room across the passage for families. Probably one of the busiest times for the little pub was during the war when it was used by Americans from nearby Dunkeswell Airfield.

It is a freehouse offering local cider and one real ale, Otter Bitter still served traditionally straight from the barrel. Brewed locally at Mathayes the Otter Brewery opened in November 1990 and is one of the Country's newest using its own spring water and local malt. The only food available are snacks like nuts, crisps etc.

The inn is open every evening except Sunday from 6.30 p.m. but more flexible during the day. Don't be deterred if the door is locked, knock hard and if she is not out shopping she will open up for you.

Children are allowed inside but there is no room for dogs.

Telephone: (0404) 891613.

Luppitt is best reached from the A30 north from Honiton.

Approx. distance of walk: 3.5 miles. O.S.Map 192 ST 169/066.

Park where you can in the village.

A challenging walk, full of interest along bridleways, through woods, across moorland, over streams and farm land. The walk also takes you through Hillend Farm where the Otter Brewery is established. The first section across Hense Moor is very demanding and really only suitable for experienced walkers; it is the spring of the Otter and consequently very wet and boggy so strong waterproof footwear is essential.

Leave the inn and turn right walking up the hill only as far as the signed bridleway on the right. Follow the track round, bearing left at the cross track then up and round taking the right fork. Keep to the level track until you reach a small dwelling on the right referred to locally as the love nest. Ahead of you is a farm gate. The footpath is shown to leave the track and head in a straight line towards the moor but has been fenced. Until the authorities waymark the exact line I suggest you bear left up the bank, pass through the farm gate at the top and head across the scrub towards the valley. There is no actual path but several obvious animal tracks, try to keep in a straight line until you reach the moor where a path twists down the bank towards the stream. At the bottom is a small wooden gate. Go through, cross the stream and follow the boggy path up the opposite hill keeping fairly close to the field boundary on the right.

Turn left at the top, and after a few paces, look for a path on the right leading up into the scrub. It is set back just behind a small parking area. The path broadens as it rises up to meet the moor after which bear right down towards the stream at the bottom. Again this path is not easy to follow. The area under foot is green sand and very boggy in places. There are many tufts of grass which make walking hard. The only advice I can give is bear half right, find a way down and at the bottom there is a an old rickety wooden bridge. If you miss it walk in either direction until you find it. I can assure you it is there. Having found the bridge cross to the far bank, bear left and then right to pick up a path which will bring you out to an open area of grass at the back of the house. Go across to the drive and turn right. The footpath is shown on the right crossing the field to the brewery but the owners would prefer walkers to carry on up the hill and enter the driveway on the right. They are in negotiation with the landowner of the field on the left to re-route the path through the farm gate directly into the field, but for now

follow the correct route down between the farm buildings.

Bear right through the gate, then left up across the grass to the farm gate in the top corner. Go into the field, bearing left across to the far hedge and make your way to the gate in the far corner. Pass through and keep straight ahead, through another gate, past the farm building and straight ahead to the stile. The path, raised at first above paddocks, crosses to a gate in the far hedge. Go through heading down towards the house and leave by the stile next to the gate. Walk round into the drive then left through the farm gate up to the lane and turn right. When you eventually reach the T junction turn right back up the lane to the pub.

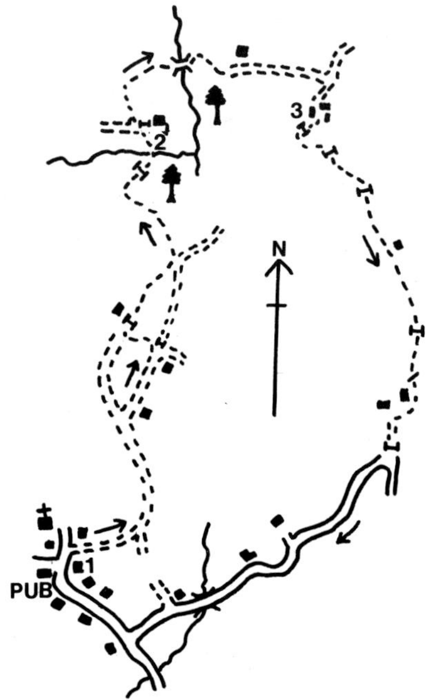

The Castle Inn, Lydford

The hidden remains of a bronze age fort suggest the area around Lydford was inhabited long before Christ and it was here that a Royal Mint was established during the reign of Edward the Martyr producing coins known as "Lydford Pennies" some of which can still be seen in the pub. Named after the castle this lovely, unspoilt 16th century Inn is one of the finest traditional pubs in Devon; if not the country.

The mostly plain, pink exterior offers no clue to what awaits you inside. The cosy bare stone walled "Tinners Bar" has two lovely open fireplaces, secluded alcoves, a polished slate floor and low bowed ceilings. A small family room is separated from the passageway by two huge curved wooden settles, but the piece-de-resistance is the charming restaurant. In the end stone wall is a great Norman fireplace housing a roaring log fire, a collection of plates hang from the beamed ceiling and there are dozens of lovely antique oil lamps. There is a covered patio at the back with more seating in the pretty gardens.

The inn is a freehouse extremely well run by the owners, Clive and Mo Walker. The well stocked bar offers a selection of wines, local cider and three real ales Palmers Bridport Bitter, Dartmoor Best and a guest ale.

Excellent bar meals are listed daily on the blackboard and on my last visit included spicy beef curry, hot and sour sizzling prawns, haddock in a cream and wine sauce with a cheese and potato topping, pork cobbler, Somerset chicken cooked in a cider sauce, mussel chowder and the inn's own very popular steak and kidney also a vegetarian dish, aubergine and red peppers with cream cheese. In the restaurant there is a set menu or a choice of dishes such as "coronation chicken" - breast of chicken, pan fried and served with a creamy port sauce and "lamb romarin" - tender fillet of lamb cooked in a sweet, brandy and rosemary sauce.

Dogs on a lead in the bar only. Weekday opening times are from 12 noon till 3 p.m. and 6 p.m. till 11 p.m. Accommodation is available.

Telephone: (082 282) 242.

Lydford Gorge

The White Lady Waterfall

Walk No. 23

Village signed from A386 between Okehampton and Tavistock opposite the Dartmoor Inn.

Approx. distance of walk: 3.50 miles. O.S.Map 191 SX 508/848.

There are no parking problems in Lydford. The inn has its own car park and there is a free public car park opposite.

The walk round Lydford Gorge is one of the most scenic if not the most dramatic in Devon. A fast flowing river with deep pools, swirling currents and dramatic waterfalls, it is owned by The National Trust and open daily, when conditions permit, from the 1st of April to the 1st of November, between 10 a.m and 5.30 p.m. The upkeep of such a beautiful spot is high and quite naturally a charge has to be made for entry - but worth every penny. In 1992 the charge was £2-60 and half price for children. It is not an easy walk but it is a safe walk providing you take care. The walk down the gorge is on a well maintained path through the trees. There are two path options down to the waterfall, a long easy route or a short but steep path with many steps. The walk back up the gorge can be very precarious underfoot but handrails are provided. Some sections are quite steep and narrow and there are lots of steps so strong well treaded footwear is essential. Access to the Devil's Cauldron is on a narrow metal walkway and no more then 6 people at any one time can view the swirling waters below. At peak times you are warned to expect a wait of anything up to an hour. I was last here on a Friday afternoon in mid August and there were just two people waiting in front of me but that would not necessarily always be the case.

Leave the pub turning right, cross the bridge at the bottom and immediately turn right into the entrance of the gorge. Tickets must first be purchased in the National Trust Shop. Pass through the shop and bear right across the picnic area to the start of the walk. The path rises high above the gorge giving the occasional spectacular glimpse of the river below. The route is quite straight forward needing little or no explanation.

After crossing the river by the waterfall entrance you have two options, a long easy route or a short steep walk down many steps. Both paths meet up again below the White Lady Waterfall. Cross the bridge and return along the lower path. There is no chance to hurry as the uneven paths are steep, narrow and slippery, but who would want to; the scenery is breathtaking and can only be appreciated at a slow pace. To avoid the cauldron and return to the car park you can cross by the Pixie Glen footbridge. A warning states that dogs are not allowed and it is not suitable for children or those of a nervous disposition.

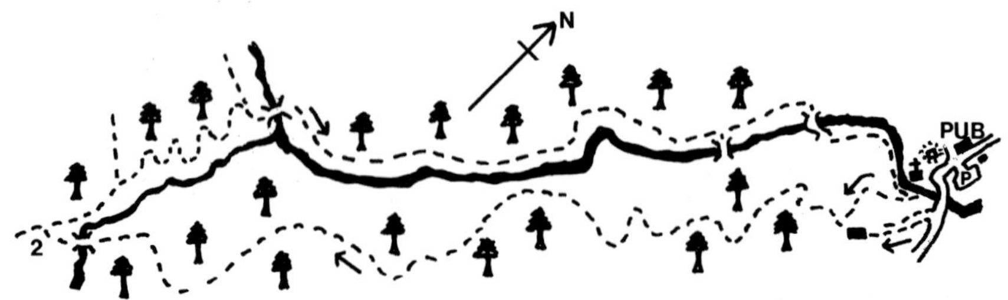

The sketch maps in this book are not necessarily to scale but have been drawn to show the maximum amount of detail.

Kestor Inn, Manaton

The Kestor Inn is in a sunny position high above the road on the edge of the village. The pub is some ninety years old and was once a small guest house owned by a local farmer. He also owned the village pub, which at that time was sited near the village green, but decided to transfer the licence to the present building. Over the years there have been many alterations to both the exterior and interior of the building. The comfortable main bar which has lots of dark wood, cosy alcoves, attractive bare stone walls and an open fireplace opens out on to a separate dining area and sunny front terrace.

The Inn is a free house beautifully kept and well run by the owners, Nigel and Alison Ford. The well stocked bar includes three real ales, Flowers Original, Marstons Pedigree and Wadworth 6X.

A very good and extensive food menu is served seven days a week although Sunday lunch time the menu is limited to a four course special. Lunchtime bar snacks include tasty ploughman's, open sandwiches, filled jacket potatoes and homemade steak and kidney pie. The main menu, supplemented by daily blackboard specials such as fisherman's pie and fresh Torbay crab, offers a tempting choice of steak specialities. "Kestor" is an 8oz steak fillet in a stroganoff style cream, mushroom, garlic and brandy sauce whilst in another variation the steak is topped with mature Stilton and walnuts and grilled until golden brown. There are vegetarian meals and two separate children's menus, one for young children and one for under 14's.

The Inn is open during the week from 11 a.m. till 3 p.m. and 6 p.m till 11 p.m. Families are welcome so too are dogs if kept on a lead and under control. Overnight accommodation is available in rooms with four poster beds.

Telephone: (064 722) 204.

Walk No. 24

The best route to Manaton is from Haytor Vale off the B3387 about three miles east from Bovey Tracey.

Approx. distance of walk: 2.5 miles O.S.Map 191 SX 757/807.

Park at the pub, in the lane outside or near the village green.

The area around Lustleigh and Manaton is excellent walking country. Both villages have their own pub, The Cleave at Lustleigh is the older being a XVth century thatched Inn. Both villages are equally attractive but Lustleigh is the busier and parking is a problem. The many footpaths and bridleways in the area are all well marked and trail guides are available listing the best of them. The walk I have chosen, although fairly short, can take a while due to the uneven ground and the steepness of some of the paths. It makes an ideal family walk through beautiful woodland and takes in the attractive Becky Falls.

Leave the inn and walk down the hill, past the lane on the left walking only as far as the gate on the left. Go through and bear right following the path close to the hedge on the right. Cross the stream and follow the main path through the woods ignoring the side paths. It is a lovely walk with lots of wild flowers. Impressive rock formations jut out high above the path and colourful lichens and mosses cling to the many bolders.

After crossing a stile the path passes close to the River Bovey then heads down towards Becky Falls. When you reach the wooden bridge bear left unless of course you want to visit the visitor centre. Further ahead at the fork deviate right, steeply down steps to the base of the falls - well worth the diversion especially if the river is high. Retrace your steps back up to the fork and turn right. Ignoring the side turnings continue ahead, over the stile, past the woods and straight ahead at the junction of the bridleway signed, Bovey Valley. Further on take the left fork, up the bank through the trees. The path then descends quite steeply to meet a bridleway at the bottom.

Turn left, and after climbing steadily through more attractive woodland carpeted with many wild many flowers the path, wet and muddy in places, passes through a gate onto a narrow track. At the top turn right on to the path and walk up to the cross track. Keep straight ahead walking around the buildings, out into the tarred lane and turn right. After passing some idyllic cottages turn right at the road junction back to the pub.

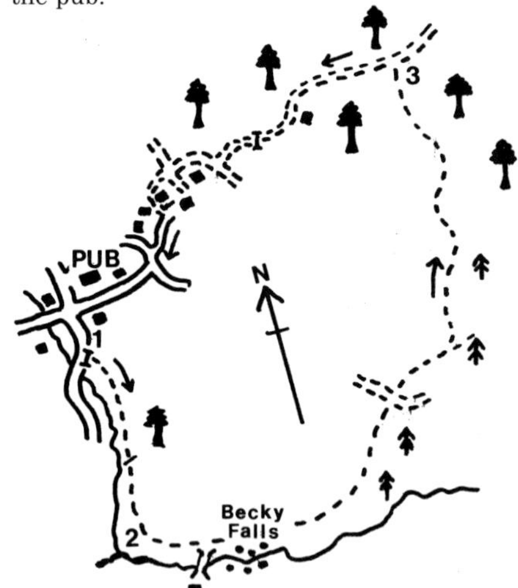

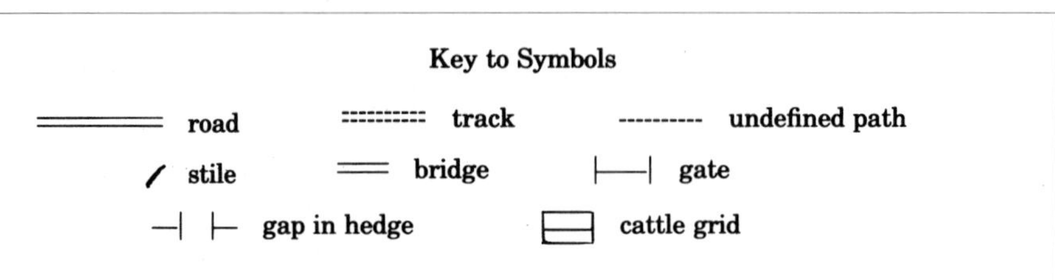

The sketch maps in this book are not necessarily to scale but have been drawn to show the maximum amount of detail.

River Bovey

Becky Falls

The Dartmoor Inn, Merrivale

Originally quarryman's cottages built in the 17th century the Dartmoor Inn was once part of the Walreddon Manor Estate. It has been a pub at least since 1852 when the record office in Tavistock was destroyed. Situated at 1000 feet above sea level the inn occupies an enviable position overlooking the Walkam Valley. On a clear evening one can see the lights of Plymouth and beyond that the flashing beam of the Eddystone Lighthouse.

It is a busy roadside inn and although altered little externally the interior has undergone change. The mostly open plan main bar has a large stone fireplace at one end housing a warm log fire in winter behind which is an additional seating and games area. The walls are bare stone and painted white with dark wood inserts. There is a separate dining room and picnic benches outside at the front. The inn is personally run by the owner, Paul Grist who took over the licence in 1987.

The well stocked bar has a large range of country wines, Countryman's scrumpy and four real ales. Worthington Best Bitter, Charrington I.P.A. Draught Bass, and Merrivale, specially brewed by Bass.

Served seven days a week the bar menu, which includes meals for children, offers a choice between homemade soup, jacket potatoes, ploughman's, salads, pasties, sandwiches, meat or vegetable lasagne and beef and kidney pie. Evening diners can pick any of five starters, seafood au gratin is one example and consists of cod, prawns and crab in a garlic and cream sauce and to follow scampi provencale, a vegetarian chilli, beef curry, pork Calvados and steak Madagascar which is fillet steak served with fresh peppers and flamed with brandy in a cream sauce. Sweets range from "Dartmoor Delight", a combination of peaches, ice cream, clotted cream and butterscotch to "Bishops Bonanza" - bananas and ice cream in a melba sauce.

Weekday opening times are from 11 a.m. till 3 p.m. and 6 p.m. till 11 p.m. Dogs are allowed in the bar on a lead. The inn has three letting rooms.

Telephone: (082 289) 340.

The inn is on the B3357 between Tavistock and Princetown.

Approx. distance of walk: 5 miles. O.S. Map 191 SX 549/752.

There is ample parking both at the front of the pub and in the old road plus several off road parking areas close by.

A fairly demanding but never the less extremely enjoyable walk. The varied route at first takes you across open moor land past granite tors then over farm land, along quiet country roads and back to the pub on a very attractive but sometimes muddy bridleway through the Walkham Valley.

Turn right from the inn up the hill and then left on to the moor opposite the entrance to Merrivale Quarry. Keep to the left of the leat walking fairly close to the stone wall, after which head up the moor to the right of Vixen Tor. Round the wall at the end, cross the stream and continue uphill until you pick up a track near the top running between the stone wall on the left and Heckwood Tor.

Bear left at the fork then left again onto the track turning right into the lane at the bottom. In fifty yards turn left, and in 200 yards enter the farm, the path is signed. At the end of the yard go through the gate on the right, into the field and bear left in the direction of the finger post across to the far top corner. Pass through the stone gateway crossing the field to the stiles in the far hedge. Immediately turn right, climb the stepped stile in the wall and continue along the right-hand field boundary until a gate allows access to a track leading up to the road.

Turn left then left again on to the stone track. At the bottom turn left in to the road by the cattle grid. After crossing the bridge the road rises very steeply up to the crossroads. Turn left, and after reaching the end of the lane, keep straight ahead through the gates on to the bridleway signed, Merrivale 1.50 miles. Needing little explanation the picturesque track, uneven in places, rises steadily through woods and between rocky outcrops. After crossing a tributary of the River Walkam, the track continues to rise through a farmstead before heading down towards the road and the pub.

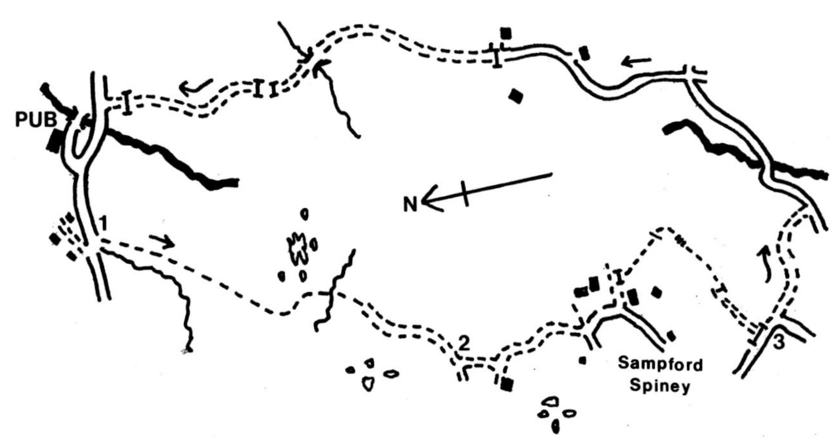

The sketch maps in this book are not necessarily to scale but have been drawn to show the maximum amount of detail.

The Ship Aground, Mortehoe

For many years the isolated community living in Mortehoe were often dependent for their livelihood on what they could salvage from the many ship wrecks in the area. These were not always as a result of the gales. A lantern tied to a cow or a donkey gave seamen far out in the channel the impression of a safe haven only to run aground on the rocks. Until the early nineteen eighties the aptly named "Ship Aground" was just a row of three cottages. A photograph taken in the nineteenth century clearly shows them in the book, TWO VILLAGES by R.F.Bidgood.

The present owner, Roger McEvansoneya, converted them into this attractive and popular inn. Lots of shipping regalia is displayed on the bare stone walls in the mainly open plan front bar and in the smaller back bar. There is a separate family room, a small front terrace and an attractive upstairs bar opening on to another sunny terrace.

The inn is a freehouse offering a choice of real ales. At present there is Exmoor Ale, Royal Wessex plus a guest such as Boddingtons Bitter.

A full range of good home cooked bar food is available all week. Apart from the usual snacks of soup, ploughman's, and sandwiches garlic mushrooms are listed together with mussels au gratin. An interesting selection of main meals include chicken chasseur, braised lamb kidneys cooked in stout, local crab and paella together with favourites like homemade steak and kidney pie, chicken curry, cottage pie and home cooked ham. Vegetarians are well catered for with a choice of six dishes ranging from vegetable lasagne to baked broccoli and cream cheese with a sliced potato topping.

Opening times are from 11 a.m. till 3 p.m. and 6 p.m. till 11 p.m, extended to 12 o'clock on Friday and Saturday evening. In the busy summer months the pub is often open all day. Families are welcome so too are dogs if kept under control.

Telephone: (0271) 870856.

Mortehoe is signed from the B3343 at Turnpike Cross south west from Ilfracombe.

Approx. distance of walk: 3.25 miles. O.S.Map No. 180 SS 457/454.

Although there is a small car park at the front of the inn it is better to use the pay car park on the left as you enter the village.

A very enjoyable, scenic coastal walk ideal for the whole family. It is not too long and although mostly good underfoot can be a bit strenuous. The lighthouse at Bull Point is sometimes open to the public.

Turn left from the inn and then left into the lane signed, to Lee and The Lighthouse. Pass through the gate and follow the drive walking until you eventually reach Bull Point, about a mile and a half in distance. On the way there is a good view down the valley to Pensport Rocks. Subject to the discretion of the keeper in charge, it is possible for members of the public to view certain part of the lighthouse on weekdays.

Turn left on to the coast path. It is well signed, easy to follow needing little explanation. Shortly after the start there is a small wooden gate beyond which are a steep flight of steps up the cliff. There is another stile further ahead. The sandy inlet on the right is Rockham Bay. Cross the next stile and take the right fork. After more steep steps fork left up the hill. Part way up a seat has been thoughtfully provided to rest awhile and enjoy the lovely view. Further on when you reach a cross path turn left and walk up the rise, through the small gate on to the track, which after passing the cemetery leads straight back to the pub.

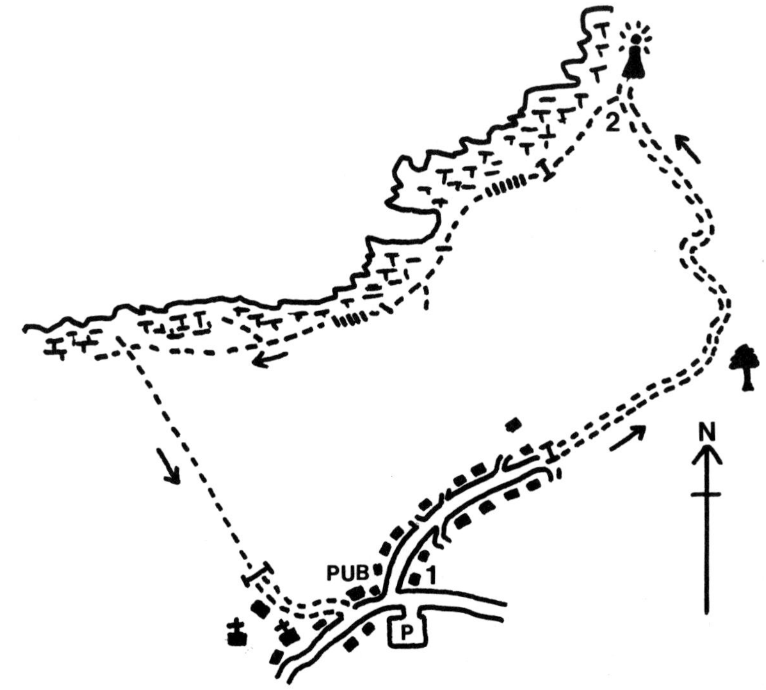

Ring of Bells, North Bovey

North Bovey is regarded by many to be one of the most picturesque and unspoilt villages in Devon. Centered around the village green, many of the thatched cottages date from the 17th century or earlier.

Pride of place though must go to the delightful thatched, Ring of Bells. Built in the 13th century, the name is derived from the church of St John The Baptist which once possessed a peel of four bells.

The warm cosy lounge, heated by a wood burning stove in the large stone fireplace, has a low beamed ceiling and wooden settles against the bulging white walls, one actually encloses an old long case clock. The bar and a separate games room are reached through a small door in the wall. There is an equally attractive restaurant on the other side of the stone entrance passage and picnic benches positioned to make the most of the sunny front garden.

The three real ales are regularly changed in this freehouse but the popular ones are Wadworth 6X, Furgusons Dartmoor Best Bitter and Ind Coope Burton Ale.

The inn has a very good reputation locally for its bar food. Freshly prepared at lunchtime there is a choice between tasty parsnip soup, traditional ploughman's, cold meat salads, steak and kidney pie, chilli and delicious lasagne. Diners in the restaurant can select snails cooked in garlic butter followed by supreme of chicken poached, with apples in a cream and cider sauce and fillet steak, sliced in three and sauted in butter with garlic, onions and tomatoes then flamed in brandy and finished with cream. Children have their own menu and there are usually at least two vegetarian meals.

Weekday opening times are from 11 a.m. till 3 p.m. and 6 p.m. till 11 p.m. There is no objection to dogs if kept on a lead. Overnight accommodation is available in four poster beds.

Telephone: (0647) 40375.

Best reached from the A382 between Bovey Tracey and Moretonhampstead. An alternative, more picturesque route is from the B3387 through Manaton.

Approx. distance of walk: 3 miles. O.S.Map 191 SX 742/838.

Park anywhere in the village or in the free car park opposite the church.

An easy walk down to the River Bovey then across farm land finally returning to the village along peaceful country lanes.

Leave the pub and turn left walking down the lane to join with the gravel track. After passing the stone building cross the stile on the left and follow the wide grass track to the top. Cross the stile into the field and, keeping close to the hedge on the right, make for the stile on the far side then bear right down to the stile by the small brook. Bearing right walk up the field to the gate in the top corner and keep straight ahead to the crossing point in the far hedge leaving the field through the farm gate ahead of you.

Cross the track and climb the stile making your way over the field to the stile in the far hedge turning left on to the track. Cross the lane into the driveway of the house, and almost immediately go over the fence into the field on the left. In the direction of the finger post walk to the corner, cross the stile and continue walking close to the hedge, over the crossing point and out through the kissing gate on to the track. Climb the stile ahead of you into the field and keep walking over another stile finally leaving in the corner on to the track. Cross one last stile into the lane and turn left.

Turn right at the road junction then left at the crossroads down the lane to the village. Although some distance back to the pub the lanes are very peaceful with little or no traffic and there are some fine views of Easdon Tor and the surrounding hills. The hedgerows are abundant with wild flowers and ferns, bright blue Borage, Pink Campion, Bluebells, Foxgloves and spikes of white Navel Wort to name but a few.

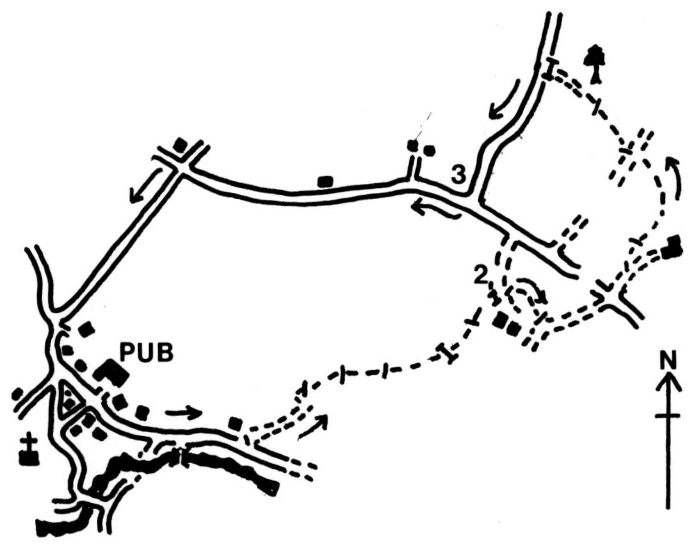

Old Ship Inn, Noss Mayo

Noss Mayo is one of my favourite places in Devon. It is a lovely picturesque village, relatively unspoilt and still much the same today as when I first came to the area many years ago. The houses in Noss Mayo and Newton Ferrers are built one above the other on the steep banks above the estuary. On a fine day there can be nothing more relaxing than to sit outside the Old Ship Inn sipping a cool drink and enjoy the view.

Starting life in the sixteenth century as a customs bond house and later two cottages it became an Inn known as The Globe but in 1966 was renamed The Old Ship. Painted white, two cosy, solid stone walled rooms have bay windows overlooking the creek. One step from the bar takes you into the family room and a flight of stairs up to the attractive restaurant. A nautical theme prevails throughout even ships port holes are built into the doors.

The inn is a freehouse well run since 1983 by the present friendly owners, Norman and Val. Well conditioned real ale is still served traditionally straight from barrels at the back of the bar. Presently there are three, Dartmoor Best, Wadworth 6X and Draught Bass. There is also a good wine list.

Tasty bar snacks include soup, sandwiches plain and toasted, ploughman's, gammon egg and chips and homemade steak and Guinness pie. In the restaurant cast off with "barnacle paint" - a crab cocktail or perhaps "ladies hole" - crispy coated cauliflower florets. "Whole rigging" is a mixed grill of steak, lamb chop, bacon, eggs, sausage, mushrooms, peas, onion rings, tomatoes and chips. Other dishes include beef stroganoff, surf and turf, lemon sole, shark steaks and scallop mornay plus vegetarians meals. On Friday evening and Saturday lunchtime a two course carvery is served greatly reduced for O.A.P's and free for children under 10.

Children are welcome in the family room and there is no objection to dogs. Weekday opening times are from 11 a.m till 3 p.m. and 6 p.m. till 11 p.m.

Telephone: (0752) 872387.

Noss Mayo is signed From the A379, 5 miles east from Plymouth at the junction with the B3186. The pub is situated on the eastern side of the small estuary and can be reached from the estuary or from the lane at the back.

Approx. distance of walk: 4.25 miles. O.S.Map 201 SX 547/476.

Park anywhere in the village, in the car park by the tennis courts or in the estuary but be careful not to park too far down and be caught by the tide.

A very scenic coastal walk on wide gravel tracks, through woods and along The South Devon Coast Path. The going is generally easy and good underfoot making it an ideal walk for the whole family.

Leave the pub by the back entrance and turn right along the single track road. After a short distance take the signed path on the left up the steps into Fordhill Plantation. Owned by The National Trust the path runs through the trees level with the lane and is a more pleasant route providing shade on a hot sunny day and cover when wet. Eventually when the path rejoins the lane, which has now deteriorated into a rough gravel track, turn left then pass through the gate.

Keep to the main track, past the cottages then through the gate onto The Warren. There is a lovely view through the valley across Wembury Bay to the prominent Mewstone. keep to the main path, crossing the occasional stile, walking round the scenic Mouthstone and Gara Points. Further on a short detour takes you on a narrow path in front of Warren Cottage.

After rounding Blackstone Point fork left up the track, pass through the gate by the car park, into the lane and turn left. In twenty paces turn right onto the rough track signed to Noss Mayo. Pass in front of the cottage following the track until it merges with a tarred lane before reaching the village. After passing the tennis courts turn left down the lane to reach the pub.

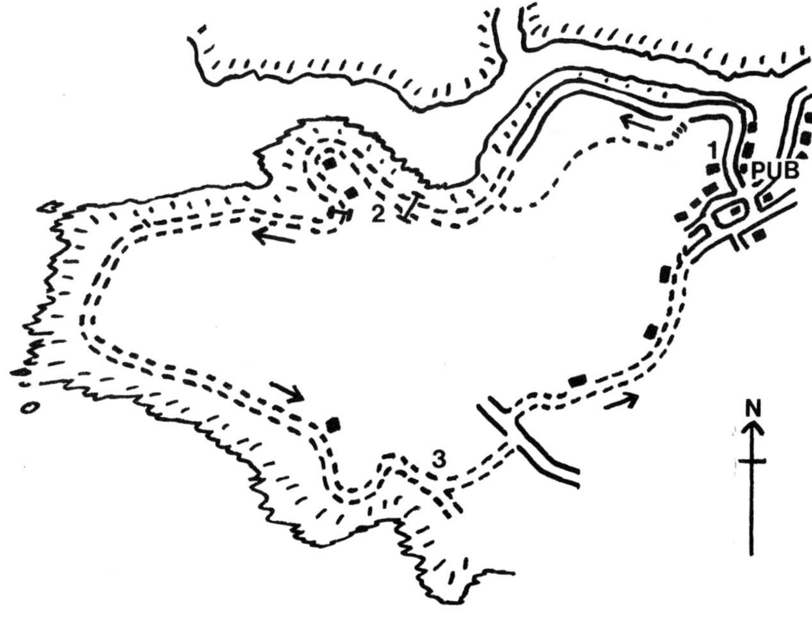

The Kings Arms, Otterton

Otterton is situated in the valley of the River Otter and much of the land surrounding the village is owned by the Clinton family as indeed were many of the houses until recently. Otterton Mill, restored in 1977 and open to the public, is the last working mill on the river. The cornmill has been grinding grain since before the Norman Conquest and the flour is still used to bake fresh bread on the premises.

Higher up the street is the village pub. Rebuilt by the Victorians in 1889 the exterior has changed little but the interior has been modernised, a painting at the time can be seen hanging above the front mantelpiece. The rooms have been knocked through to form one large open plan bar with a central servery. The floor is warmly carpeted and the walls are both bare brick and painted with lots of light wood in evidence. There is a log effect gas fire serving one half of the pub but a traditional log burning stove on the other side nearest to the bar. A separate room doubles as a skittle alley and family room and there are lots of picnic benches in the beer garden.

The inn is a freehouse presently offering a choice of two real ales, draught Bass and Flowers I.P.A also Palmers Traditional cider.

In addition to sandwiches, ploughman's and chef's soup the menu lists a selection of home cooked meals such as steak and kidney pie and sausage platter. Also a separate children's choice. "Todays Catch", chalked daily on the black-board except Monday, might offer skate wing, a very large cod fillet or whole plaice. Other specials could include beef stroganoff, chicken breast with Stilton and mushroom sauce and for vegetarians a vegetable chilli or mushroom and nut fettucine. Pineapple crumble and toffee apple sponge are just two of the tempting sweet choices.

Weekday opening times are from 11 a.m. till 3 p.m. and from 5.30 p.m. till 11 p.m. Telephone: (0395) 68416.

From the A3052 turn south on to the A376. Otterton is signed just before reaching the village of East Budleigh.

Approx. distance of walk: 6 miles. O.S.Map 192 SY 082/853.

Park either in the car park or anywhere in the village street.

This popular walk at first heads down to the shore along the banks of The Otter, then follows the South Devon Coast Path to Ladram Bay before returning on an attractive network of paths leading directly into the rear garden of the pub. It is a fairly long walk but easy going for most of the way.

Turn right from the inn, and after passing the mill, cross the river and immediately turn left through the kissing gate following the path beside the river. Many wild flowers grow along the banks notably masses of the late summer flowering pink Himalayan Balsam. Follow the river through several gates until a minor road is reached then turn left over the river and bear right through the farm gate to join The South Devon Coast Path signed, Ladram Bay 3 miles.

After reaching the coast the path climbs away from the estuary and then continues to rise and fall for some distance. Several stiles later you reach Ladram Bay. It is worth just going down to the beach to see the red cliffs and stacks. You can also buy fresh shell fish from a fisherman's shack.

Walk a few steps up the lane and rejoin the path on the left signed, To Otterton ¾ of a mile. After rising through a gully the path crosses a field and continues up to merge with a track. At the junction with another track turn right and then left into the lane.

In thirty yards pass through the kissing gate on the right and cross the field to the gate at the top of the rise. Walk beside the hedge until you reach the stile then follow the path down to the lane and turn left. Turn first right into the bus turning area and keep straight ahead on the grass track, past the thatched cottage then bear left following the path up to the stile. Cross into the field, then go left into the adjoining field and make your way down to the stile following the path into the back garden of the pub.

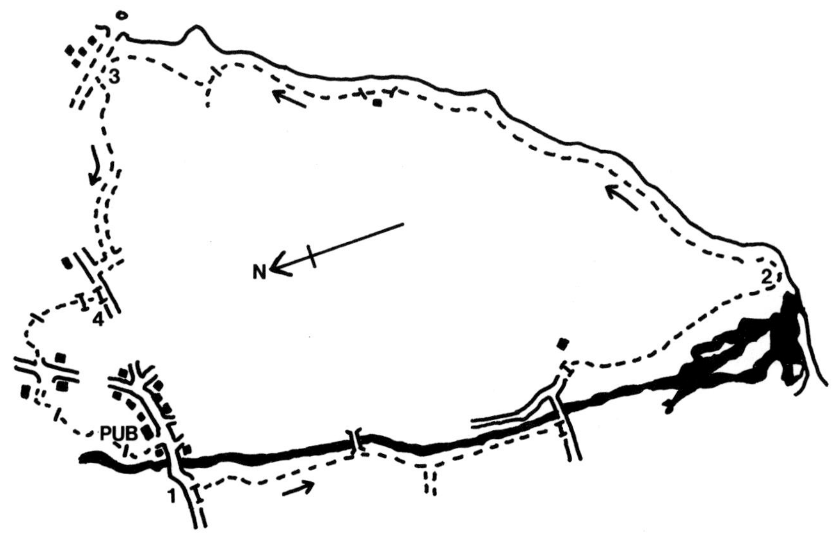

The sketch maps in this book are not necessarily to scale but have been drawn to show the maximum amount of detail.

Fox and Goose Inne, Parracombe

For three hundred years there has been a pub on this site but it was burnt down in 1892. The present Victorian building was completed in 1894 by Henry Robert Blackmore, the second cousin of Richard Dorridge Blackmore the author of Lorna Doone, and formed part of the Blackmore Estate. The pub is very much a village local. The large main bar is simply furnished with country style chairs, tables and padded settles and heated in winter by an open fire. Lots of hunting regalia decorate the walls and there are several old photographs including one showing the original two storey thatched pub. There is a pool room and a separate cosy dining room with slate top tables and an old grinding wheel displayed in the centre of the room.

The inn has always remained a freehouse and is well run by the present owner. Real ale is still served traditionally straight from the barrel. Out of season there is usually just the one, the prize winning Burton Ale, but at other times there can be anything up to six or seven.

The extensive bar menu is diverse in style with something to suit all tastes. Served seven days a week and chalked on the blackboards above the bar the list includes Ploughman's, home made soup, corn on the cob, mushrooms cooked in wine, cream and paprika, half a pint of prawns with a garlic dip and homemade pate. "Foxy fry up" is sausage, egg, bacon, beans, fried bread and chips. There are various omelettes, battered squid rings, breast of chicken sauteed in white wine and mushrooms, various steaks and a gander grill. Specialties include local oak smoked trout and home made shepherds pie. There are several fish dishes like lemon sole poached in butter also barbecued shark and swordfish steaks.

Weekday opening times are from 12 noon till 3 p.m. and 6 p.m. (7 in the winter) till 11 p.m. Well behaved children are welcome also dogs on a lead.

Telephone: 05983 239.

Village signed from the A39, 4 miles west from Lynton.

Approx. distance of walk: 3.5 miles. O.S.Map 180 SS 668/449.

Although the pub has its own car park it is fairly small and the owners are not keen on people parking there unless actually using the pub. Better to drive on through the village and up the hill into the recreation area on the right. There is space for about five cars.

An enjoyable walk along peaceful country lanes into the Heddon Valley then up a track beside the Heddon River and back across farm land. Although hilly in places the going is fairly easy underfoot apart from the last track which can be a little uneven and wet in places.

Turn left from the inn and continue though the village, up the lane until you reach a short track on the left leading to a stile beside a gate. Go into the field walking to the far hedge. Cross both stiles then follow the rough track across the field to the gate. Keep straight ahead beside the hedge and leave by the wooden gate on to the farm road, turn right and then left into the lane.

It descends quite steeply between fields into a very attractive wooded valley. Many wild flowers grow from the lush roadside verges. After about a mile, and just beyond the ford on the right, look for a gravel track on the left. A sign indicates, Heddon Valley Mill Luxury Holiday Cottages. The track rises steadily close to the River Heddon.

After crossing a couple of cattle grids, fork left following the track which soon narrows to a path then rises quite steeply up to gate leading into an open field.

Walk straight ahead, keeping fairly close to the hedge on the right, pass into the field and continue walking, through another field gap and across to a bridleway. Go through the small gate in front of you, cross to the far side of the field and leave through the gate onto the track. It is fairly wide, a little uneven in places and sometimes wet underfoot. Pass through the gate into the lane following it back down to the village turning right for the pub or left to the picnic area.

Peter Tavy Inn, Peter Tavy

This charming inn lies in The Dartmoor National Park on the eastern side of the River Tavy. It is an old Inn dating from the 15th century and although a new dining area has recently been added it has in no way spoilt the originality of the pub. Heated by an open log fire the one low beamed bar has a timeless air. There are simple high back settles on the stone floor and window seats built into the stone walls.

The inn is a freehouse very well run by the owners Phil and Jan. Well conditioned beer is still served traditionally straight from barrels at the back of the bar. There is usually a good choice which might include Boddingtons Bitter, Palmers Bridport Bitter, Adnams Broadside and Flowers Original.

The inn is very popular for its excellent food and justifiably so. Whilst bar snack like homemade soup and ploughman's are on the menu the choice is predominantly between fish and vegetarian dishes like creamy cashew nut fingers, butter bean, leek, sweetcorn and mushroom pie, crepes stuffed with spinach and garlic, spicy vegetable crumble and Peter Tavy crunchy nut pasta. Fish dishes include langoustines pan fried in garlic and Mexican red snapper baked with banana in a sauce of peanut oil, onion, red and green pepper, white wine and parsley. Turbot is served with a prawn and crab sauce and barracuda grilled with garlic butter. In the restaurant you can order stuffed squid, seafood thermidor - scallops, scampi and crab meat cooked in white wine and coated with a creamy cheese sauce, gunard cooked with a sweet and sour ginger sauce and for sea food gargantuans the Peter Tavy Special - an enormous seafood platter for two people but 24 hours notice is required.

Families are welcome in the small snug at the front and dogs are allowed in the bar. Weekday opening hours are form 11.30 a.m. till 2.30 p.m. and 6.30 p.m. till 11 p.m. with some all day opening if business justifies.

Telephone: (082281) 348.

Peter Tavy is signed north of Tavistock from the A386 at Harford Bridge.

Approx. distance of walk: 4.50 miles. O.S.Map 191 SX 513/777.

There is a small car park at the front of the inn, a larger car park at the back and some space in the lane.

A scenic walk from this old Dartmoor mining village which at first takes you across farm land high up on to the moor beneath Cox Tor. After crossing a tributary of the River Tavy the path joins with a track close to Stephens' Grave before making a gradual descent back to the village. Although steep in places the walk is not over demanding and mostly good underfoot.

Turn left from the inn then right at the junction and left into the lane. Follow it up and round until you reach a stile on the left. Climb the bank, and bearing right in the direction of the finger post, cross the fields and boundaries leaving by the gate at the top and turn left into the lane.

In one hundred yards go through the metal gates on the left and follow the signed bridleway straight ahead up the field keeping fairly close to the wall. After passing through the gate take time to look back over you shoulder at the lovely view of the surrounding villages. After passing through another gate and reaching the stone wall, bear right at the finger post, across to the gate on the far side of the field and turn left onto the moorland road.

In a short distance, where the road dips and bears left towards a farm, continue straight ahead on to the wide grass area to pick up the wall on the left. Bear left after the corner and cross the moor making for a gate part way along the wall, the bridleway is signed. Bear right to the far corner turning left at the finger post, pass through the gate, cross the stream and head up the moor. There is no defined path but just keep walking until you eventually reach the gravel track close to Stephens' Grave then turn left.

George Stephens, a penniless labourer from Peter Tavy, was found dead on Longstone Moor the morning after a quarrel with his lovers family. No one really knows if his death was an accident or suicide. His grave is marked by an upright granite stone on a square granite base marked with an S. From here it is downhill all the way. The rough track soon merges with a tarred lane making walking easier. At the road junction turn left and in a few steps turn right onto the short track leading to the church. The narrow path ahead leads straight back to the pub.

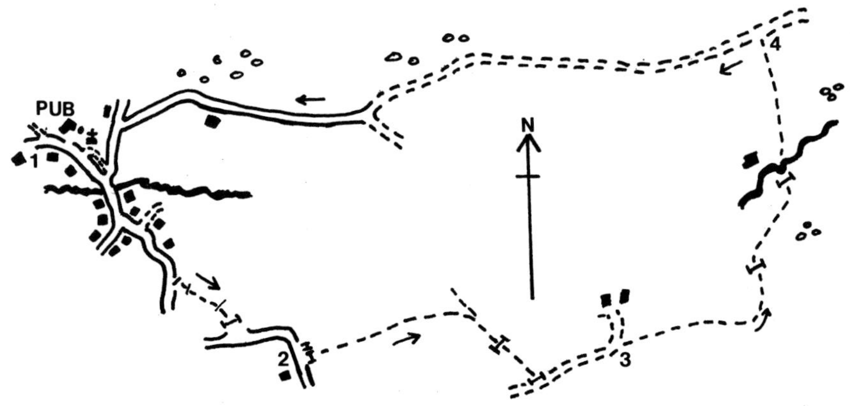

Tavistock Inn, Poundsgate

The Tavistock Inn is well over 700 years old and as far back as any records go has always been an inn. According to legend in 1638 the devil called here on his way to Widecombe. He paid for his drink with gold coins which after he left turned to dry leaves.

The lovely timbered interior of this unspoilt Dartmoor inn remains much the same today as those bygone years. The floor is part flagstoned, the walls part panelled and painted white. A unique spiral stone staircase runs up over the larger of the two stone fireplaces where there is a warm log burning stove in winter. The old stables are now an attractive family room and the pub's attractive beer garden regularly wins awards for the lovely floral displays.

Owned by Ushers the inn is very well run by the friendly proprietors, Ken and Janice Comer. Two real ales presently available are Courage Best and Ushers Best in addition Ushers new ale, "Founders" will shortly be introduced.

Meals are cooked and prepared fresh to order between 12 noon and 2 p.m, and from 6 p.m. in the evening. Each day on the menu there is a tasty homemade soup also crispy potato skins filled with ham, mushrooms and cheese. Always popular is the "Dartmoor Breakfast" - sausages, eggs, bacon, beans, bubble and squeak and toast. There is a curry a good choice of grills, fisherman's pie, a choice of freshly baked pizzas and six vegetarian specialities.

Weekday opening times are from 11 a.m. till 3 p.m. and 6 p.m. till 11 p.m. Children are allowed in the side room and dogs in the bar if kept on a lead.

Telephone: (036 43) 251.

Leave the A38 south of Ashburton and take the Widecombe road through the River Dart Country Park.

Approx. distance of walk: 2.5 miles. O.S.Map 191 SX 704/722.

As the car park opposite the inn is fairly small the licensees would prefer walkers not to park during opening hours unless of course they are visiting the pub. Ample parking is available on the moor before reaching the pub.

Although only a short walk it is certainly one of the most enjoyable in the book. After entering a field by an attractive brook a track leads down to a footpath which crosses a field to Lower Town. The walk then proceeds down a delightful country lane, crosses the brook and heads back up through an attractive wood.

Leave the pub and turn left carefully walking down the lane as far as the footpath beside the stream on the right. It is signed, Lower Town and Townwood Cottages. Follow the path ahead, round the edge of the field to the metal gate, go out on to the drive and turn right. keep straight ahead bearing left past the dwellings until you reach the finger post on the right directing you up a short track to a farm gate. Keep straight across the field to the gate, go through and bear left alongside the field boundary, through a couple more gates and out into the lane at Lower Town.

Turn right and follow the lane for just over a mile until you reach the cottage by the river. The lane is very peaceful carrying little or no traffic it is also extremely beautiful. It crosses a stream and passes beside attractive woodland. Everywhere there are wild flowers Bluebells, dozens of Primroses, garlic smelling Ransoms, Violets, Foxgloves, Pink Campion and a host of different ferns.

After crossing the bridge turn right, go through the gate and follow the track as it rises steadily through mixed woodland close to the brook. In the spring there are thousands of white Wood Anemones, Primroses and a lovely show of Bluebells. At the top go over the stile into the field and head straight across to the metal gate. Continue walking beside the hedge, through another gate and up to the stile beside the gate. Go over on to the drive and keep straight ahead retracing your steps to the metal gate then back across the field to the lane turning left to the pub. As the road can be very busy at times it is advisable to keep to the right-hand side.

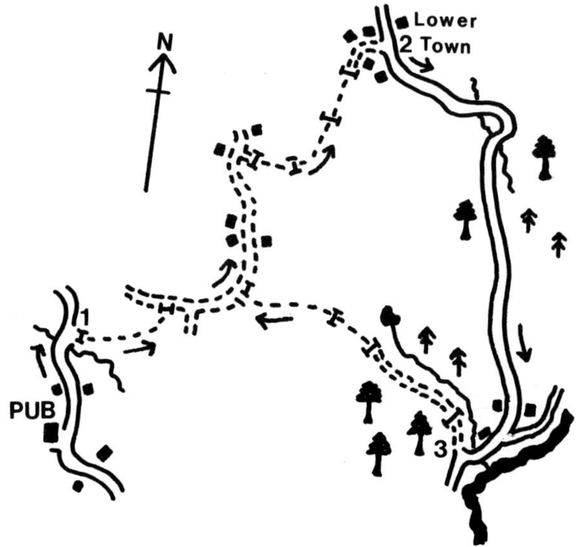

Journey's End Inn, Ringmore

As soon as I am in Devon I like to leave the busy main roads and travel slowly along the narrow winding lanes, their high hedgerows crammed in late spring with large drifts of wild flowers and to visit remote villages like Ringmore. This lovely thatched village lies in the rolling hills of South Devon just inland from the sea. Despite some recent housing the village remains unspoilt, as does the delightful village pub the aptly named Journeys End Inn.

Believed to date from the 13th century all that has changed is the name when it was known up until the 1920's as the New Inn. The ancient, beamed bar has heavy part panelled stone walls, cut down beer barrels on the flagstone floor, padded wall seats and an open fire in the raised hearth. To accommodate more people the original yard has now been converted to a comfortable wood panelled lounge with an open fire and a new sunny conservatory added at the back. There is also a large beer garden.

The inn is a freehouse very well run by the amiable landlord, Richard Sully. Well conditioned real ale is still served traditionally straight from the barrel. There is always a good choice like Smiles Best Bitter, Palmers I.P.A. Wadworth 6X, Adnams Broadside and Royal Oak.

Good home cooked bar food is freshly made every day of the week. Supplemented by daily specials such as leek and Stilton pots, moussaka and quiche and game pie, the menu features tasty soup, basket meals, sandwiches, jacket potatoes and ploughman's. Also omelettes, homemade chilli, lasagne and various steaks. Children have their own menu.

Weekday opening hours can be flexible but normally the inn opens around 11 a.m. till 2.30 p.m. and 6.30 p.m. (7 p.m. in the winter) till 11 p.m. Children are welcome away from the bar and there is no objection to dogs. Overnight accommodation is available most rooms having en-suite bathrooms.

Telephone: (0548) 810205.

To reach this lovely isolated Devon village leave the A379, between Kingsbridge and Modbury, on to the B3392 and take the sharp right-hand turn at St Ann's Chapel in front of the Pickwick Inn.

Approx. distance of walk: 4 miles. O.S.Map 202 SX 652/459.

Park at the top of the village opposite the church and walk down to the pub.

A lovely walk through a scenic valley to Arymer Cove then along the coast path and across Challaborugh Bay to Bigbury-on-Sea. The half way refreshment stop is the lovely Pilchard Inn on Burgh Island. Walk across the sands at low tide or take the sea tractor. The present charge for adults is 50p and 25p for children. The path then crosses fields and a stream before reaching the village. The going is mostly good underfoot, but strenuous in places.

Turn right from the inn walking a few steps down the lane to join the signed footpath. Turn left into the lane, pass the farm buildings and fork left onto the track. Look for a signed footpath into the field on the left and follow the path down towards the sea crossing the stile beside the gate then go through the gate on to the cast path and turn left.

Cross the bridge and follow the path steeply up the cliff to Toby's Point where you have a lovely view of Burgh Island. Continue along the coast path down to Challaborough Bay. In early summer there is a magnificent show of wild flowers in the fenced area on the left. Cross the bay in front of the caravan park and walk up the path ahead passing through the gate onto the tarred lane. At the top bear right onto the path signed, To Burgh Island, or continue along the lane. To miss seeing The Pilchard Inn would be to miss a bit of history. Built in the 14th century this delightful atmospheric inn is a little gem in Devon's crown and conveniently open all day from 11 a.m. till 11 p.m.

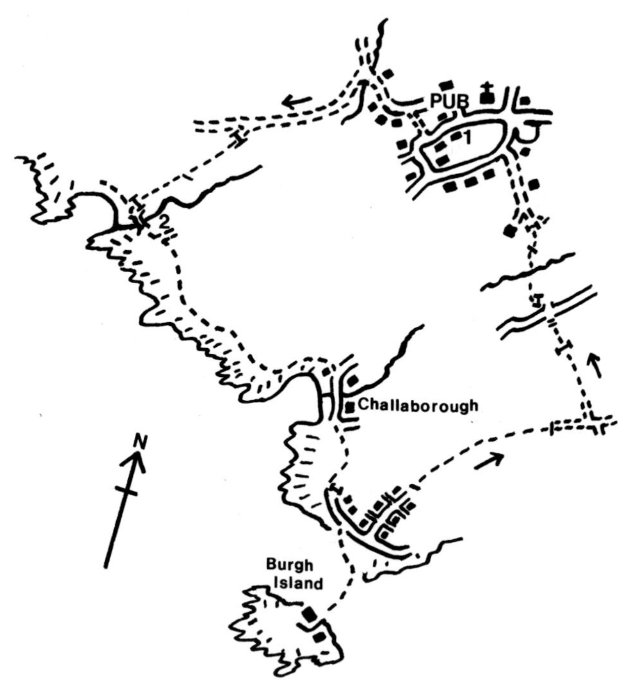

From the coast road head inland up Parker Road. Cross the stile into the field at the top, and further on pass through the gate, turning left at the finger post. Follow the short track and enter the field on the right. Walk down, over a couple of stiles and through the gate at the bottom. Head up the field to the stile, cross the lane and pass through the metal farm gate into the field on the left. Walk to the bottom, cross the stream and, keeping close to the hedge on the right, make your way up to the stile and into the adjoining field turning left. Pass through the metal gate and continue up to the stile, over on to the tarred drive, up to the road junction and turn left. The lane on the right, Just beyond the telephone box, will take you straight back to the inn.

Burgh Island

The Pilchard Inn

The Tower Inn, Slapton

Slapton is a lovely little village and although only half a mile from the coast it is miles way away from the hustle and bustle of life today. Pretty cottages bedecked with flowers are crowded together on the narrow streets. In 1372 the College of Chantry Priests was consecrated; today all that remains is the tower and within its shadow the beautiful Tower Inn.

The lovely old fireplace is just one feature in the main bar of this ancient inn, the ceilings are low, pictures and other interesting artifacts are displayed on the stone walls and seating is in comfortable low back wooden settles. The other bar, originally the cellar and similar in appearance, has a bare stone floor and an open fireplace. There is a separate family room, a restaurant and picnic benches on the terraced back lawn.

The inn is a freehouse famous for its excellent range of well kept real ales. There are usually at least six to choose from such as Wadworth 6X, Palmers I.P.A, Royal Oak, Tanglefoot, Bishops Tipple and Exmoor Ale.

The inn specializes in Italian food including pizzas with the emphasis on seafood but traditional snacks like ploughman's and baked potatoes are also on the menu. Popular pasta dishes include lasagne, spaghetti bolognese and Gorgonzola pasta which is cream and Gorgonzola in a cheese sauce whilst deep fried Camembert is served with a fruity dip. Heading the list of blackboard specialities are "Ammatriciana" - tomato sauce with chunks of ham, "Saltimbocca" - chicken breast topped with bacon and cheese and "Risotto Pescatore" - a seafood rice dish with tomato sauce, prawns, king prawns and mussels. "Tower special" is a luxurious seafood pasta of tomato sauce with prawns, mussels king prawns and crab claws. Vegetarians are well catered for and children have their own menu.

Weekday opening times are from 11.30 a.m. till 2.30 p.m. and 6 p.m. till 11 p.m. The inn has no objection to dogs if kept on a lead.

Telephone: (0548) 580216.

Walk No. 34

Slapton is best reached from the A379 coast road south from Dartmouth at Slapton Sands.

Approx. distance of walk: 2 miles. O.S.Map 202 SX 821/451.

Parking can be a problem in Slapton. The small car park at the inn holds about a dozen cars with only limited parking in the village. The alternative would be to park at Slapton Sands.

A short but extremely enjoyable walk across farm land to Slapton Ley - a remarkable fresh water lake. A board walk then allows you to cross the marshes to reach the nature trail beside the Ley. It is an ideal walk for all the family on well maintained footpaths and along peaceful country lanes.

Leave the pub, walk out into the lane and turn right. In twenty or so paces turn left following the narrow street down through the village and take the left fork. Cross the lane onto the track opposite walking until you reach a stile beyond which is a narrow footpath leading down to Slapton Ley.

Turn left onto the board walk and follow the attractive path as it winds its way across the marshes to meet with a track. Turn right following the sign to Slapton Sands. One path runs beside the waters edge the other slightly higher up the bank. It is a lovely walk, well signed and good underfoot with just the occasional stile. The path runs beside the reed beds before reaching the gate. At 500 acres the Ley is the largest natural body of fresh water in South West England making it a good natural habitat for insects, fresh water fish and birds.

Turn left into the lane keeping to the right-hand side where there is a pavement and grass verge as far as the entrance to the caravan site. Continue ahead to the village centre, turning right onto the Totnes road and following it past the church of St. James The Great, back round to the pub.

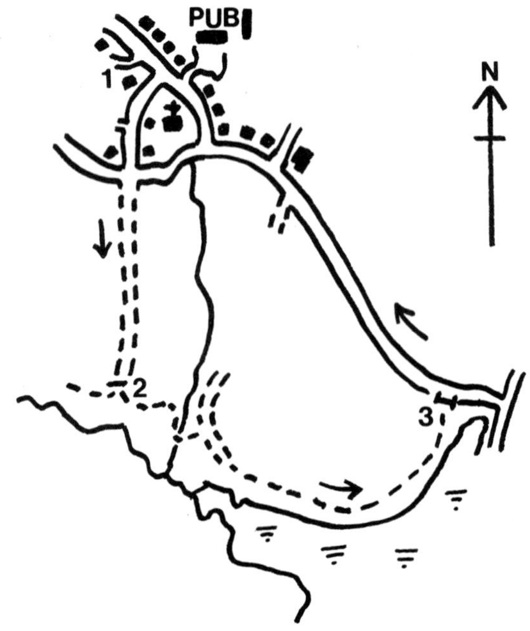

The Kings Arms Inn, Stockland

The delightful, thatched Kings Arms is an old coaching inn dating from the 16th century. The beautiful main bar, divided by an ancient wooden screen, has bare stone walls, a low beamed ceiling and heated by two open fires, the larger in a lovely inglenook fireplace which stretches almost the width of one end wall. Furnishings are mostly comfortable high back wooden settles and heavy bench tables. There is a similar very attractive restaurant, a family room which adjoins the flag-stoned bar at the rear, a skittle alley and seating in both the small front and rear gardens.

The inn is a freehouse beautifully kept and efficiently managed by the owners and staff. The well stocked bar offers a choice of three real ales, Badger Best, Ushers Best Bitter and Exmoor Ale.

Famous locally for its excellent food, the pub attracts diners from miles around so much so that it is essential to book in the evenings. Served seven days a week except Sunday lunchtime, everything is home cooked on the premises under the personal supervision of the owner, Heinz Kieferand. Chalked daily on the blackboard the selection ranges from snacks of soup, sandwiches and ploughman's to dishes such as smoked trout and mackerel, Brie in filo pastry and gravad lax. Fish features strongly with Membury trout, king prawn thermidor, darne of salmon in lobster and dill sauce and mussels when in season. Two popular dishes are supreme of chicken Jerez which is flamed in brandy, poached in sherry and reduced with thick cream, and salmis of wild duck - roasted in the oven and served with a sauce made from the carcass, liver and red wine. Alternatively you can have it slow-roasted and basted with orange and soy sauce till crispy.

Well behaved children are welcome so too are dogs. Opening times are from 12 noon till 3 p.m. and 6.30 p.m. till 11 p.m. Overnight accommodation is available. Telephone: (040 488) 3661.

Walk No. 35

Stockland is in the east of the county signed from the A35 between Honiton and Axminster and from the A30 Honiton to Chard road.

Approx. distance of walk: 3.5 miles O.S.Map 192 ST 245/047.

Park at the rear of the inn or in the lane at the front.

A very enjoyable scenic walk mostly across farm land and along peaceful country lanes. Although hilly in places it is not over demanding but can be very muddy underfoot.

Turn left from the inn and then right into the short lane to the church. Follow the path round to the left, out into the lane and turn right. Upon reaching the farm turn left on to the signed footpath along the muddy track, through the gate and across the field bearing right to the gate. Go through and aim left making your way to the hedge. Cross the ditch and head up the field, through the gap in the boundary hedge to the gate in the far top corner.

Turn right into the lane and then left at the junction. Just before reaching the stream at the bottom of the hill turn right into the rather boggy area of grass and continue straight ahead keeping fairly close to the stream. After crossing the plank bridge follow the raised path until you reach the dwellings then turn left and look for the little gate just past the house on the right. Go through and follow the raised path beside the stream, across the stile into the field, straight ahead to a second stile and out through the gate.

Turn right into the lane and almost immediately turn left on to the narrow footpath that is signed through the hedge. After crossing the footbridge turn right into the field, and keeping close to the hedge, walk round to the gate, up to the lane and turn right. Almost immediately turn left into the lane, and after passing the farm buildings, go through the gate into the field on the right. Walk across in the direction of the finger post making for a gap in the hedge boundary. Climb the bank into the field then bear left across to the gate, go through and turn right, through the gate ahead of you and across the field leaving by the small gate in the hedge.

Turn left and then right on to the farm track. Keep straight ahead through the farm gate and make your way across the field to the stiles in the far hedge. Cross into the field, and keeping close to the hedge, walk round passing through the open gateway down to the track in the corner and through North Hill Farm. Bear right on to the track and in twenty yards take the signed footpath on the left. After passing through the gateway head up the field in the direction of the finger post making for the gate in the far hedge, you will see the waymark on the gatepost. Pass through into the field and, keeping close to the hedge, bear right up to the crossing point and turn right into the lane.

After about a mile you come to a gate leading into a level field on the right. Head straight across to the gap in the hedge and walk down to the small gate in the corner. Continue down beside the hedge, through the gate at the bottom into the field and straight ahead to the farm gate in the far hedge. Bear right behind the houses to the gate, turn right into the lane then right again back to the pub.

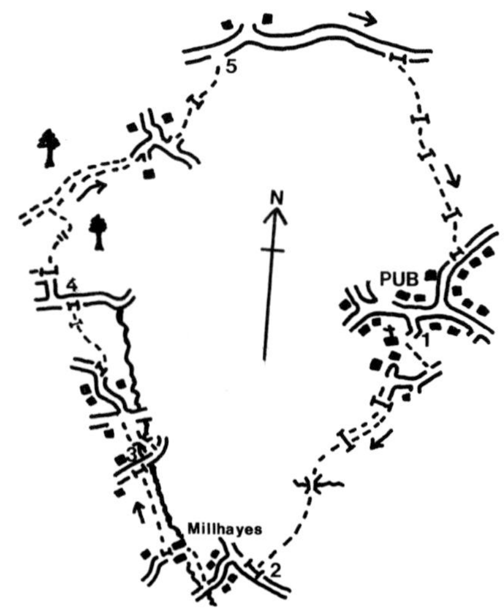

The Church House Inn, Stokeinteignhead

The name Stokeinteignhead is derived from stoke meaning a settlement, teign the old word for ten and head which is a part, hence a settlement in ten parts. Although bounded by Shaldon and the busy towns of Newton Abbot and Torquay, Stokeinteignhead and the surrounding villages still remain nicely rural.

The lovely Church House Inn dates from the 13th century and although alterations have taken place the main bar remains relatively intact. The beautifully panelled and part stone walls, the large stone fireplace, the part flagstoned floor and heavily beamed ceiling all combine to create the old world atmosphere. There is more seating by the servery beyond the archway, an attractive restaurant up a flight of stairs, a separate public bar and a small beer garden at the back. Everywhere is beautifully kept with lots of brightly shining copper items on display.

The inn is owned by Heavitree who used to brew their own beer in Exeter but is now run by Badger Inns. A warm welcome is assured from the friendly manager, Jim Wilson. Presently there are three real ales, Draught Bass, Boddingtons Bitter and Thomas Hardy Country Bitter.

The bar menu which includes a choice of ploughman's, soup, pasta in vegetable mornay, salads, Church House pie, gammon and nachos - a bowl of spicy chilli served with tortilla chips is supplemented by daily specials such as crumbed turkey breast filled with Camembert and served with cranberry sauce, fresh plaice toped with prawns in a mornay sauce and sausage and spicy red wine casserole. Also a selection of children's meals.

From Easter through till the end of September the inn is open all day from 11 a.m. till 11 p.m, but closes for the rest of the year between 3 p.m. and 5.30 p.m. Children are only allowed in the upstairs dining room or the garden and dogs only in the public bar.

Telephone: (0626) 872475.

Walk No. 36

The village is signed from the Newton Abbot to Shaldon road at Combeinteign-head but best reached from the A379 north from Torquay.

Approx. distance of walk: 4.5 miles. O.S.Map 202 SX 915/705.

Park in the lane opposite the pub or in the car park at the rear.

A very scenic walk at first through a small wood and along peaceful country lanes leading to the coast. After following the Devon South Coast Path the route back to the village is down a steep, stoney track. Although mostly good underfoot the walk is very demanding in places especially along the coast path where there are lots of steep steps.

Leave the inn, walk up the lane opposite and in twenty yards turn right up the stoney track. Part way up take the path on the right into the trees and upon reaching the track turn right. Turn left onto the track at the bottom and further ahead pass through the kissing gate leading into the estate road and keep straight ahead up to the lane turning left.

Follow the lane for ¾ of a mile until you reach the main road. Walk straight across down Steep Hill, past the attractive Thatched Tavern and turn left in front of the car park onto the coast path signed, To-

Labrador Bay. The path, although fairly demanding, is quite straightforward and easy to follow. At times there are magnificent views along the coast. Follow the path for just over a mile until you reach a stile then head inland up to the main road and turn right.

Carefully walk along the road for a couple of hundred yards and then turn left up Commons Lane. Turn left at the top on to the stoney track, past the trig point in the hedge on the left and fork left where the track divides. At the bottom turn right into Deane Road back down to the pub.

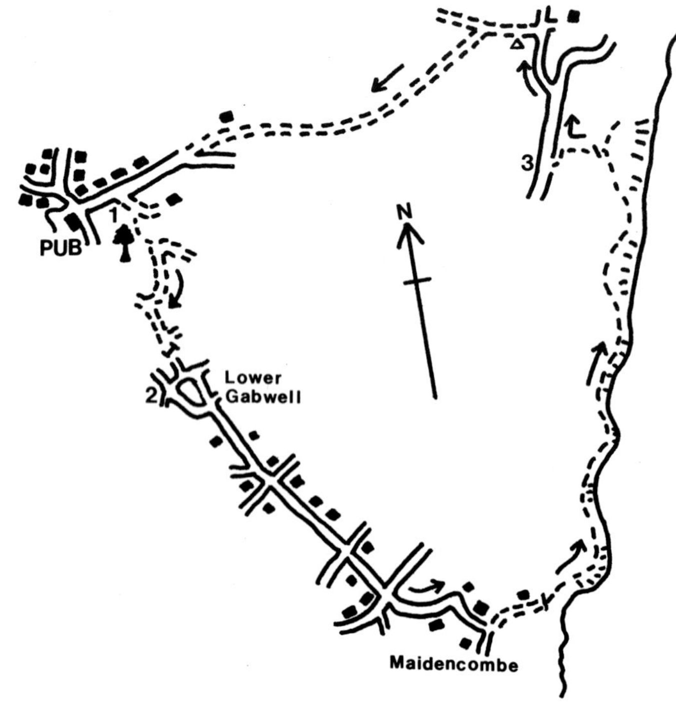

The Old Church House Inn, Torbryan

Years ago Torbryan was on the main stage route from Plymouth and was once a thriving market town. Built around the year 1400 The Old Church House Inn, like other similarly named pubs, was first constructed to house workman re-building the church. Beer was brewed on the premises and it had its own bakery. Few ancient pubs have survived so relatively unscathed into the 20th century.

Although the original entrance is now blocked up the Saxon door still survives. The lovely room behind it, mellow with age, has a low beamed and boarded ceiling and a massive step in inglenook fireplace. The main bar could not be more original it too has a low darkened ceiling, a large inglenook fireplace and heavily panelled walls. There is more seating behind the bar in the old cellar room and at the other end in the stable. The whole pub is beautifully kept and lovingly cared for but still manages to retain that lovely lived in feel, a faint aroma of wood smoke hangs in the air whilst a pile of fuel in the hearth is ready for the next fire.

The inn is a freehouse owned by the Pimm family since 1984. Real ales are traditionally still served from barrels on the bar. There is usually a choice of five or six such as Church House light, and Church House Dark, Flowers Original and I.P.A. and Brains Dark.

Cuisine is mixed but the emphasis is on traditional English food. From the excellent menu you have the choice of eleven starters like garlic mussels with prawns or prawn and mushroom crepe. There are steaks from the griddle, fresh fish and dishes such as Devonshire pheasant and lamb cutlets. Each day there is an extensive mouth watering selection of dishes on the blackboard and a tempting list of sweets ranging from pineapple melba to chopped meringue with a blackcurrant filling.

Weekday opening times are from 12 noon till 2 30 p.m. and from 7 p.m. till 11 p.m. Families are welcome. Superb accommodation is available in en-suite bedrooms.

Telephone: (0803) 812372.

Torbryan is a delightful little hamlet remotely situated in South Devon. The best route is to take the turning for Ipplepen, from the A381, between Totnes and Newton Abbot.

Approx. distance of walk: 3 miles. O.S.Map 202 SX 820/668.

Park in the lane at the front or the small car park opposite.

A lovely country walk at first across open farm land to the pretty village of Broadhempston then along a peaceful country lane and back on a field track through a delightful lush valley. Whilst it can be muddy the going generally is good underfoot.

From the pub turn left up the track, pass through the gate into the field and walk down to the gate at the bottom. Squeeze through the gap in the wall, cross the stream ahead of you and bear right over to the stile in the hedge. Make your way up the field aiming for the stile in the hedge just beyond the corner, go over and turn left up the narrow path to the stile. Cross the lane and pass through the gate into the field bearing right in the direction of the finger post but all the time walking uphill to reach the stile in the far hedge. Go over into the field following the path close to the right-hand hedge boundary then pass through the gap into the field ahead and continue across to the stile. Follow the narrow path up between the houses to the lane and turn right.

Either keep to the lane, turning right at the crossroads to Denbury, or for a longer more interesting walk, turn left into Broadhempston, then right at the T junction and right again to rejoin the lane at the crossroads. The main street down through the village is very attractive and there is always The Coppa Dolla inn if you are in need of refreshment. At first the lane descends to the valley and after crossing the stream rises quite steeply between farm land bounded by attractive stone walls. After rounding the bend keep walking until you reach the fingerpost on the right.

Climb the stone stile and bear right across the field making for the wooden stile in the far fence, cross the grass to the drive and turn left. Keeping to the right of the house, pass through the gate into the field following the grass track straight ahead, through a couple more gates before arriving back to the village.

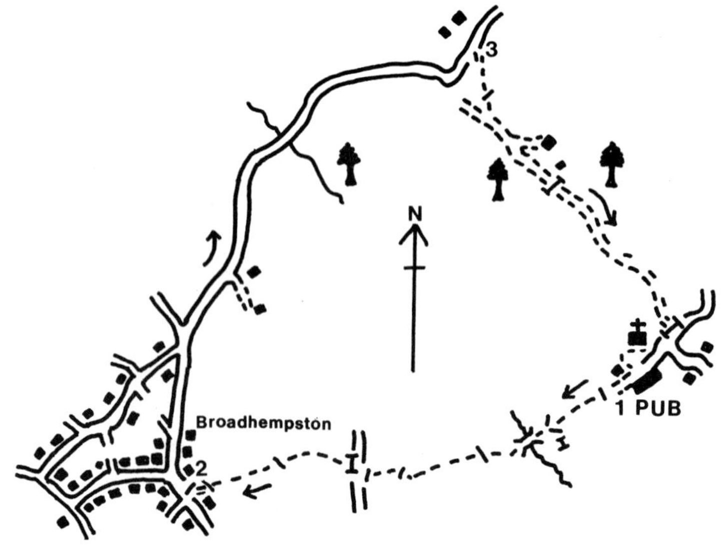

The Coppa Dolla Inn

Marsland Mouth, Welcombe

The Old Smithy Inn, Welcombe

For such a remote spot as Welcombe it was indeed a real pleasure to find the delightful, thatched Old Smithy Inn not known to be before. This friendly, family run pub, originally an ale house before becoming the local smithy and later a farmhouse, re-opened as an inn in 1962. From the thatched entrance porch one enters directly into the cosy low beamed bar. There is a separate restaurant and a paved terrace at the front with seating. The gardens are beautifully kept and would be of interest to families as there are several aviaries containing geese, chickens and owls rescued from the wild by the owners son who is a trained falconer.

The inn is a freehouse very well run by the resident owners, Geoff and Sandra Marshall. Two well conditioned real ales presently available are Butcombe Best Bitter and Marston's Pedigree.

The lunchtime bar menu, served from 12 noon, is the typical pub fare of sandwiches, ploughman's, baked potatoes, soup of the day, Cornish pasty, various grills and local steak and kidney pie, whilst the restaurant menu offers more variety. To start there are barbecued spare ribs and calamari, followed by sweet n sour chicken, lasagne and honey roast duck in orange sauce. Children have their own menu and vegetarians can choose from pasta helena, vegetable lasagne or garlic mushrooms.

The inn is open all day from 10.30 a.m, when coffee is served through till 3 p.m, for afternoon tea. The inn closes at 5.30 p.m. for half an hour re-opening at 6 p.m. There is no objection to dogs. Overnight accommodation is available.

Telephone: (028 883) 305

Welcombe is just a small hamlet in the extreme east of the county signed from the A39.

Approx. distance of walk: 3 miles. O.S.Map 190 SS 232/178.

The inn has its own car park.

After a lovely walk down to the coast at Marsland Mouth the return route takes you through a most attractive wood to Gooseham Mill and up a picturesque track.

Leave the pub by the front entrance into the lane and turn right. There are two path options, the easiest being to keep to the narrow lane which is very peaceful and attractive then bear left at the double junction and left again at the T junction. If you wish to avoid the lane take the signed footpath down the track on the left. Bear right in front of the derelict building and pass through the gate into the field on the right. Keeping close to the hedge walk straight ahead to the crossing point and continue ahead to the far boundary. Again cross over into the field ahead and, bearing slightly left, make your way towards the stone buildings. A narrow path, signed with white arrows, directs you to the right, between the buildings and out into the lane.

Turn left, and in fifty paces, turn right on to the signed footpath to the right of the house. At the end of the track pass through the gate into the field and continue down to the stile on the cliff top. Turn left, cross the stile ahead and follow the path as it dips down towards Marsland Mouth. After a long flight of steps the path joins with another before reaching the valley.

Turn left and head inland to join the track beside the cottage. After climbing steeply and passing through a farm gate the track meets up with the road. A footpath is signed through the farm gate on the right. Pass through and follow the well worn path down, across the meadow until you reach a stile beside a gate. The path beyond takes you through a most attractive wood to Gooseham Mill just crossing the border into Cornwall. There are many wild flowers to be seen notably Primroses and many attractive ferns.

Climb the stile and follow the path up to the driveway, turn right and then left into the lane. Cross the bridge back into Devon and head up the track. It is muddy at first, a little uneven and quite steep in places. Keep to the main track and eventually when you reach the lane at the top turn right back to the pub.

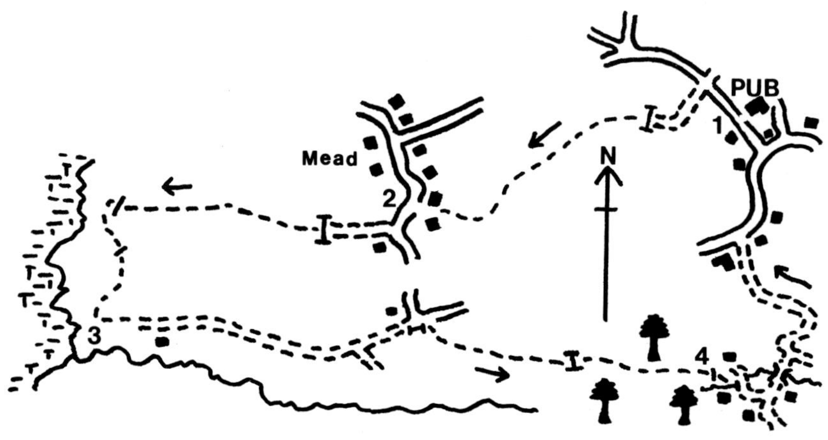

The sketch maps in this book are not necessarily to scale but have been drawn to show the maximum amount of detail.

Rugglestone Inn, Widecombe in the Moor

There cannot be many people who have never heard of Widecombe. We all learnt the song at school about "Uncle Tom Cobley and all" going to Widecombe Fair. The fair is still held here on the second Tuesday in September but is now in the form of a gymkhana with demonstrations and sideshows. The centre of this lovely Dartmoor village is dominated by the church of St Pancras. The 120 foot tower, the second tallest in Devon, can easily be seen from the surrounding downs. Each year thousands of visitors descend upon this small community, many of them probably unaware of the existence of the charming Rugglestone Inn.

Completely unspoilt it is one of the few original pubs still left in Devon. Built from local stone some two hundred years ago it occupies a quiet, sunny position surrounded by fields with a small stream passing the front door. It has always been a simple pub owned up until August 1992 by Miss Lamb who lived there all her life. Happily the new owners, Lorrie and Moira Ensor, still intend keeping it that way and extend a warm welcome to walkers. Two rooms lead off from the stone entrance passageway both similar in character with bare stone floors, exposed ceiling beams, warm open log fires and a mix of old tables and chairs, one of them has an interesting high back wooden settle. Seating is provided outside and in the field at the front.

Local farm cider and well kept Draught Bass, kept in the cellar room on the opposite side of the passage, is still served traditionally straight from the barrel.

A limited snack menu is available which includes rolls, pasties, sandwiches, ploughman's and hot soup in the winter.

Licensing restrictions do not permit children anywhere inside the inn but there is no objection to well behaved dogs. Weekday opening times are from 11 a.m. till 2.30/3 p.m. and 6 p.m. till 11 p.m.

Telephone: (036 42) 327.

Follow the B3387 from Bovey Tracey or head north from the A38 at Ashburton. Widecombe is well signed.

Approx. distance of walk: 7 miles. O.S.Map No. 191 SX 720/767.

As parking is limited at the pub a field is often opened in summer to alleviate the situation but there is no problem in the village especially as there is a free car park opposite the church.

A fairly long but most enjoyable scenic walk which takes you high up across the moor, past ancient barrows and down to Grimspound - a Bronze Age settlement which dates from about 1500 BC to 500 AD. It is an easy going walk, and although a little uneven in places is mostly dry underfoot.

From the inn walk back to the village centre, turn right and then left on the road to Natsworthy. Further ahead take the signed bridleway on the left. The lane rises very steeply to join with an uneven track which brings you on to the open moor. Continue ahead to the finger post, bear right and follow the track to the boundary wall. Keeping close to the wall, walk to the far corner and then head up on to the moor. When I was last here in 1992, a new route was signed due to path erosion.

At the top continue along the broad ridgeway, past Two Barrows and Single Barrow, then fork left at Broad Barrow up to Hameldown Beacon, 1,735 feet high and marked by a triangulation point. Bear left and head down the moor to Grimspound. This Bronze Age pound is one of Dartmoor's most interesting monuments and one of the oldest dwellings on the moor. From the stone circle bear right and follow the wide track around the moor, down past woods on the left, across the stream, out through the gate into the lane and turn right.

It is a very attractive and peaceful lane back to the village. Part way down you can shortcut the corner across the field by Lower Natsworthy Farm and further down, if you still have the energy, take the track on the left just beyond the cattle grid. It rises steeply up round Chinkwell Tor. When you reach the road bear right through Bone-

hill back down to the village. For my part I prefer a leisurely stroll to the village back down the lane.

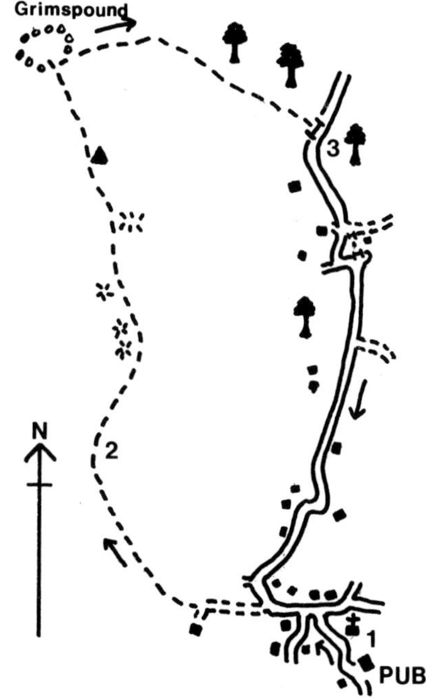

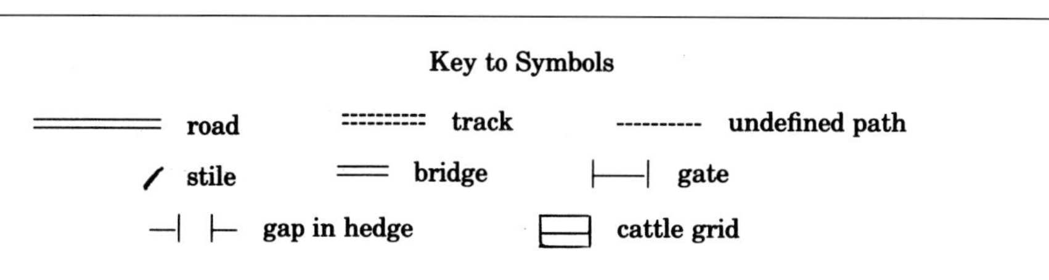

Key to Symbols

════ road	┈┈┈ track	------- undefined path
╱ stile	══ bridge	├──┤ gate
─┤ ├─ gap in hedge	▭ cattle grid	

The sketch maps in this book are not necessarily to scale but have been drawn to show the maximum amount of detail.

Widecombe in the Moor

A Dartmoor pony grazing on the moor above Widecombe

The Diggers Rest, Woodbury Salterton

Up until 1955 this lovely thatched pub was just a cider house known as The Salterton Arms but was aptly renamed after its Australian landlord. The building itself is at least 500 years old and although alterations have been carried out the essential old world atmosphere has been preserved.

From the front door one enters directly into the beautifully decorated main bar. Heated by an open fire in winter it has a low, dark beamed ceiling throughout with an ancient wooden screen separating a smaller seating area at one end. Window seats are built into the thick stone walls whilst in one corner a small area of the floor has been cut out to accommodate an impressive grandfather clock. The old stable block is now the public bar with pew style wooden benches, there is a separate skittle alley and a pretty terraced garden at the back.

The inn is a freehouse very well run since 1957 by the owner Sally Pratt. Three real ale presently available are Draught Bass, Flowers I.P.A. and the award wining Dartmoor Best.

Very good food, all homemade on the premises, is served daily from 12 noon till 1.45 p.m and from 7 p.m in the evening. Daily specials like trawler pie, cauliflower cheese with smoked bacon, steak and kidney pie, tetrazzini - turkey cooked with pasta in a sherry sauce and sweet and sour pork offer an interesting alternative to the bar menu which includes the standard fare of sandwiches, ploughman's and jacket potatoes. Also available is a tasty homemade curry, hot turkey pie, sirloin steak, various salads and at least two vegetarian meals.

Weekday opening times are from 11 a.m. till 2.30 p.m. and 6.30 p.m. till 11 p.m. Children are welcome with their parents but only if dining in the end room. Dogs are allowed in the public bar on a lead.

Telephone: (0395) 32375.

Walk No. 40

Village signed south from the A3052 between Exeter and Newton Poppleford.

Approx. distance of walk: 3.5 miles. O.S.Map 192 SY 013/890.

Park at the back of the pub or in the lane at the front.

An easy going walk along peaceful country lanes and across open farm land.

Turn left from the pub and then bear left past the cottage. Carry on along the lane until you come to the right hand bend then turn left onto the track. It is signed to Higher Pilehayes and The Mallards. Follow the track up to the bend and keep straight ahead into the field beside the entrance to the house. Stay close to the hedge on the left walking down to the stile, cross into the field and continue down to the stile at the bottom. After negotiating the plank bridge head up the field to the gate at the top. Continue following the hedge on the right to the stile in the corner of the field, cross the lane and the stile into the field opposite. Keeping close to the hedge boundary walk up to the gap in the hedge pass through and turn left onto the rough track, walk up to the lane and turn right.

In two hundred yards turn left on to the track next to the house. Immediately go over the stile into the field on the right and turn left. Follow the path down beside the hedge over the stile and then across the field to the gate. Leave by the stile and turn left into the lane following it round to the road and turn left.

Carry on up the hill, past the lane on the right until you reach the stile beside the gate on the right. Go into the field, turn left and make your way round to the stile in the far corner, cross into the adjoining field and turn right. Keeping close to the hedge walk round to the stile, cross the plank bridge into the field and bear left to the stile in the hedge. Continue in the same direction crossing two stiles and a plank bridge finally leaving by the gate into the lane. Walk straight across into the lane opposite. There are lots of wild flowers to be seen growing in the hedgerows especially Primroses. Turn left at the junction, keep straight ahead at the crossroads then turn right in the village back to the pub.

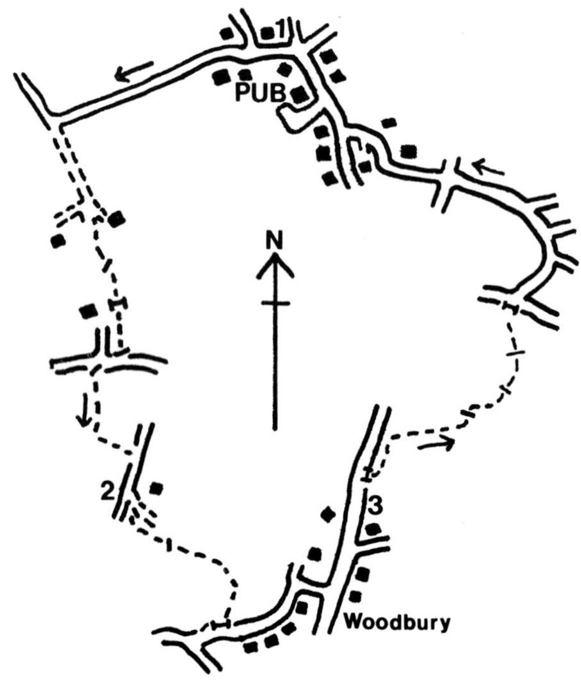